C000292424

Paines Plough in a co-production with Soho Theatre presents

roaring TRADE

by Steve Thompson

This play was originally commissioned by Paines Plough Theatre Company and produced in a co-production with Soho Theatre. It was first performed at Soho Theatre, London on 7 January 2009, directed by Roxana Silbert.

Celebrating 40 years of new writing at Soho Theatre 1969-2009.

Paines Plough in a co-production with Soho Theatre presents

by Steve Thompson

CAST
(In order of appearance)

Jess **Phoebe Waller-Bridge**
Donny **Andrew Scott**
PJ **Nicolas Tennant**
Spoon **Christian Roe**
Sean **Jack O'Connor**
Sandy **Susan Vidler**

Writer **Steve Thompson**
Director **Roxana Silbert**
Designer **Kandis Cook**
Lighting Designer **Wolfgang Goebbel**
Sound Designer **Matt McKenzie**
IT & Media Designer **Matt Kirby**

Production Manager **Matt Noddings**
Deputy Stage Manager **Eavan Murphy**
Assistant Stage Manager **Zelie Pereira**
Wardrobe Supervisor **Carrie Bayliss**
Assistant Director **Laura Keefe**
Assistant Designer **Alison Neighbour**

Casting Director **Nadine Rennie**

Press Consultant **Clióna Roberts on 020 7704 6224**

Set built by **Rupert Blakeley**

With thanks to Speakerbus, Boris Boskovic, Tracy Letts, Luke Norris, David Thompson.

JACK O'CONNOR SEAN

Jack is 13 years old and lives in Pinner Middlesex. He has trained at the Barbara Speake Stage School in Drama, Dance and Singing since the age of 4. Theatre includes: **The Snowman** (The Peacock Theatre London, Manchester and Birmingham). Television includes: **Holby City, Casualty, Living It, Skins**. Film includes: **The Thread** with Saffron Burrows and Jimmy Mistry. He would love to say a big thank you to his family, his school and his chaperone Sheelah for their continued support.

CHRISTIAN ROE SPOON

Christian graduated from LAMDA in 2008. Theatre includes: **Diary of a Madman, Richard III, Fathers and Sons, Still, The Seagull, The Pillowman** (LAMDA); **Ask and Tell, Shakespeare In The Square, Murder in the Cathedral** (NYT); **Charley's Aunt** (British Touring Shakespeare); **The Marowitz Hamlet** (Strange Bedfellows); **Hey! Mr Producer** (Lyceum Theatre); **Oliver!** (London Palladium). Television includes: **Wallander, Walter's War**.

ANDREW SCOTT DONNY

Theatre includes: **Sea Wall** (Bush Theatre); **The Vertical Hour** (Broadway, Drama League Award nomination); **Aristocrats** (National Theatre, Theatregoers choice nomination); **Dying City, Girl In A Car With A Man** (Olivier Award); **Crave, Playing The Victim** (Royal Court); **Original Sin** (Sheffield Crucible); **The Cavalcaders** (Tricycle Theatre); **The Coming World** (Soho Theatre); **Dublin Carol** (Old Vic/Royal Court Downstairs); **Lonesome West** (Druid/Royal Court); **Long Days Journey Into Night** (The Gate, Dublin, Spirit/Independent Award); **The Secret Fall Of Constance Wilde** (Abbey Theatre/Barbican, RSC); **The Marriage Of Figaro, A Woman Of No Importance, Six Characters In Search Of An Author** (Abbey Theatre); **Brighton Beach Memoirs** (Andrews Lane Dublin). Film includes: **The Duel, Little White Lie, Dead Bodies** (IFTA Award, Shooting Star Award, Berlin Film Festival) **Cigarette Girl, Nora, Longitude, Saving Private Ryan, Sweetie Barrett, Miracle At Midnight, Drinking Crude, Korea**. Television includes: **John Adams, Nuclear Race, The Quatermass Experiment, My Life In Film, The Plot To Kill Hitler, This Is Dom Joly, Band Of Brothers, The American, Budgie**. Radio includes: **Life of Chekhov, Romeo and Juliet, The Charterhouse Of Parma, Tender Is the Night, Barry Lyndon, Dubliners**, all for BBC.

NICOLAS TENNANT PJ

Theatre includes: **Romeo and Juliet** (Middle Temple Hall); **Piranha Heights** (Soho Theatre); **People at Sea** (Salisbury Playhouse); **Caucasian Chalk Circle, The U.N. Inspector, The Blue Ball, Billy Liar, The Associate** (National Theatre); **Under the Black Flag** (The Globe); **Member's Only** (Trafalgar Studio); **Dead Funny** (West Yorkshire Playhouse); **Dr Faustus** (Liverpool Playhouse); **Love Me Tonight** (Hampstead); **Cloud 9, Billy Budd, Teeth 'N' Smiles** (Sheffield Crucible); **The Taming of the Shrew, The Tamer Tamed, King Lear** (RSC); **Christmas Carol, The**

Recruiting Officer (Chichester Festival Theatre); **Comedians** (Oxford Stage); **Action** (The Young Vic); **Herons** (Royal Court); **Les Justes** (Gate Theatre); **Little Malcolm & His Struggle Against the Eunuchs** (HTC); **Sugar, Sugar, Love & Understanding** (The Bush Theatre); **New Play Festival** (Derby Playhouse); **Henry VI (I & II)** (English Touring Theatre and Old Vic); **Not a Game for Boys** (NOT the National Theatre tour & Edinburgh Festival); **Bad Company** (National Theatre Studio and The Bush Theatre); **Sailor Beware** (Queen's Theatre Hornchurch and tour); **Soundings** (Old Red Lion); **Inventing A New Colour** (Northcott Theatre Exeter); **K-Top** (National Theatre Studio). Television includes: **Terry Pratchett's The Colour of Magic & Hogfather, Residents, Eastenders, Back-Up, The Bombmaker, Between The Lines, Friday On My Mind, Nice Town.**
Film includes: **Sex Lives of the Potato Men, Tube Tales, Oscar & Lucinda, Backbeat, The Gift, The Fool, A Dangerous Man.**

SUSAN VIDLER SANDY

Theatre includes: **Nobody Will Ever Forgive Us** (National Theatre Of Scotland/ Traverse Theatre); **Petrol Jesus Nightmare** (Traverse Theatre/Kosovo Festival, Best Actress Award Kosovo International Festival 2006); **A Thousand Yards** (Southwark Playhouse); **Ju Ju Girl** (Traverse Theatre); **Sabina, Trainspotting, The Present** (Bush Theatre); **Heartless** (ICA London); **A Better Day** (Stratford East). Film includes: **A House In Berlin, Fallout, Voices From Afar, Poppies, Wilbur Wants to Kill Himself, Baby Blue, The Present, Trainspotting, Naked.** Television includes: **Stacked, Hustle, Rebus, The Last Detective, Terry McIntyre, The Jump, Impact, Love In The Twenty First Century, Kavanagh QC, The Woman in White, Macbeth On The Estate, Stone Cold, Flowers Of The Forest, Dark Adapted Eye, England Expects, Cracker, Alone.**

PHOEBE WALLER-BRIDGE JESS

Phoebe is a graduate of RADA. Theatre includes: **Twelfth Night** (Sprite Productions); **Crazy Love** (Paines Plough); **Is Everyone Ok?** (nabokov); **Rural** (White Bear/Box of Tricks); **Tales From Ovid** (Traumwand Projekt). Film includes: **The Reward, Lost Hearts, Perfect World.** Phoebe is Co-Artistic Director of DryWrite (www.drywrite.com).

KANDIS COOK DESIGNER

Theatre includes: **Romeo & Juliet, Twelfth Night, Noughts & Crosses, A New Way To Please You** (RSC); **It's A Mad World My Masters** (Globe Theatre); **Portia Coughlan** (Abbey Theatre Dublin/Royal Court); **Pale Horse** (Royal Court); **Tartuffe** (Abbey Theatre, Dublin); **The Last Days Of Don Juan, Luminosity, Epiceone, Bite Of The Night, Arden Of Faversham** (RSC); **Richard II, Loves Labours Lost** (Royal Exchange); **The Relapse** (Lyric Hammersmith); **The Promise** (Liverpool Everyman); **Dr Faustus** (Lyric Hammersmith/Fortune Theatre); **Berenice, Britannicus** (Lyric Hammersmith); **Hamlet** (Donmar Warehouse/Piccadilly Theatre); **The Crucible** (Leicester Haymarket); **The Faith Healer, The Grace Of Mary Traverse, Women Beware Women** (Royal Court); **Lucky Strike** (ICA). Ballet includes: **Marie Antoinette** (premiering 2009), **Velocity, The Four Seasons** (Houston Ballet); **Tribute To Ashton** (ROH Linbury Studio); **Cupid & Psyche** (Royal Danish

Ballet); **Powder** (BRB); **Turn Of The Screw** (London Royal Ballet); **Garden Of Joys & Sorrows** (Arc Dance Company); **Taiko** (San Francisco Ballet); **Fingerprints** (Cincinnati Ballet); **Queen Of Spades** (Les Grands Ballets Canadiens). Opera includes: **Orlando** (Wexford Opera Festival). Film includes: **Duet, Piano Tuners of Earthquakes, Sandman**. Musicals: **Mit Eventyr** (Gladsaxe Theatre, Denmark). Costumes only: **Death In Venice** (premiering 2009, Staatsoper Hamburg); **The Orpheus Suite, Pulcinella** (BRB); **Medea** (Opera North); **Orpheus In The Underworld** (ENO); **Julius Caesar, Antony & Cleopatra, King Lear, Beauty and the Beast, Henry IV Part 1 & 2, Henry V** (RSC); **The Tempest** (RSC Tour UK, Hungary, Japan & USA).

WOLFGANG GOEBBEL LIGHTING DESIGNER

Wolfgang has worked all over the world in theatre, dance, new music and opera, with artists from diverse disciplines and backgrounds. In opera he has worked with companies from Berlin, Tokyo, San Francisco, Houston, New York City, Dallas, London, Paris, Geneva, Barcelona, Moscow, Athens, Rome, Milan, Turin, Munich, Frankfurt, Stuttgart and Hamburg. Additional plans for '09 include: **Lucia di Lammermoor** (Brussels); **Die Tote Stadt** (Royal Opera House); **Let 'Em Eat Cake** (Opera North); **Meistersinger** and **Traviatain** (Cologne); **Aida** (Floating Stage, Bregenz); **Eliogabalo, Norma, Cunning Little Vixen** (Grange Park Opera Festival).

MATT KIRBY IT & MEDIA DESIGNER

Matt trained in Drama and Technical Theatre Arts at Middlesex University. His roles have included lighting design, video design, technical management and computer programming. Having worked as Studio Manager for the Young Vic Theatre and Technical Manager for the Bush Theatre, Matt now works for ICT Partnerships providing IT consultancy and technical support for London theatres and production companies. Matt also ran Paper Props, a company providing bespoke graphic designs and physical props for theatre, film and TV. Theatre credits include: **Saucy Jack and the Space Vixens** (West End) Prop Design; **As You Like It** (West End) Prop Design; **Whipping It Up** (Bush Theatre/UK tour/West End) Video Design; **How To Lose Friends and Alienate People** (West End) Prop Design; **Got To Be Happy** (Bush Theatre) Computer Programming; **The God Botherers** (Bush Theatre/New York) Prop Design; **Don Juan** (Lyric Hammersmith) Prop Design; **Damages** (Bush Theatre) Prop & Video Design; **Oliver Twist** (Lyric Hammersmith) Prop Design; **Age Of Consent** (Bush Theatre) Lighting Design; **Sakina's Restaurant** (Bush Theatre) Lighting Design; **A Carpet, A Pony and a Monkey** (Bush Theatre) Prop Design; **A Dark River** (Young Vic/UK tour) Video Design.

MATT MCKENZIE SOUND DESIGNER

Matt came to the UK from New Zealand in 1978. He toured with Paines Plough before joining the Lyric Theatre Hammersmith in 1979, and then Autograph Sound in 1984. Theatre work includes: **Wuthering Heights** (Birmingham Rep); **Flamingos, Damages, After The End, tHedYsFUnCKshOnalZ** (Bush Theatre); **The Seagull, Master and Margarita, 5/11, Babes In Arms, Funny Girl, Music Man** (Chichester Festival Theatre); **Frame312, After Miss Julie** and **Days of Wine and Roses** (The Donmar); **Sweeney Todd, Merrily We Roll Along** (Derby

Playhouse); **The Giant** (Hampstead); **Three Sisters on Hope Street** (Liverpool Everyman); **Angry Housewives, The Way of the World, Ghost Train** (Lyric Theatre Hammersmith); **Family Reunion, Henry V, Hamlet, The Lieutenant of Inishmore, Julius Caesar, A Midsummer Night's Dream, Indian Boy** (RSC); **Leaves of Glass, Baghdad Wedding** (Soho Theatre); **Iron, The People Next Door** (Traverse); **Made in Bangkok, The House of Bernarda Alba, A Piece of My Mind, Journey's End, A Madhouse in Goa, Gasping, Tango Argentino, When She Danced, Misery, Things We Do For Love, Long Day's Journey Into Night, Macbeth, Sexual Perversity in Chicago, A Life in the Theatre, Nicholas Nickleby** (West End); **Amadeus, Lysistrata, The Master Builder, School for Wives, A Streetcar Named Desire** (for Sir Peter Hall). He was also Sound Supervisor for the Peter Hall Seasons at The Old Vic and The Piccadilly and designed the sound for **Waste, Cloud 9, The Seagull, The Provok'd Wife, King Lear, The Misanthrope, Major Barbara, Filumena, Kafka's Dick.**

ROXANA SILBERT DIRECTOR

Roxana is Artistic Director of Paines Plough and has recently joined the RSC as Associate Director. She was Literary Director at the Traverse Theatre (2001-2004) and Associate Director, Royal Court (1998-2000). In 1997, Roxana was Associate Director of West Yorkshire Playhouse where she directed **Precious** by Anna Reynolds. For Paines Plough: **After The End** (Traverse, The Bush, 59e59, international tour); **Strawberries in January** (Traverse); **Long Time Dead** (Plymouth Theatre Royal/Traverse); **Shoot/Get Treasure/Repeat** (Village Underground/North Wall/Latitude); **Being Norwegian, Between Wolf and Dog** (Shunt Vaults/Òran Mór); **Under My Skin** (Òran Mór); **Dallas Sweetman** (Canterbury Cathedral). For the Traverse: **The Slab Boys, Still Life** from The Slab Boys Trilogy; **The People Next Door** (Transferred to Theatre Royal, Stratford East); **Iron** (Transferred to Royal Court); **15 Seconds, Green Fields** and **Quartz**. For the Royal Court: **At the Table/Still Nothing, I Was So Lucky, Been So Long, Fairgame, Bazaar, Sweetheart, Mules**. Other recent theatre includes: **Under The Black Flag** (Globe); **Whistle in the Dark** (Citizens Theatre, Glasgow); **Blonde Bombshells** (West Yorkshire Playhouse); **Property** (RNT Studio); **Damages** (Bush Theatre); **Brixton Stories** (RSC); **Fast Show Live** (Hammersmith Apollo/tour); **Splash Hatch on the E Going Down** (Donmar Warehouse); **The Treatment** (Intercity Theatre, Festival, Florence).

STEVE THOMPSON WRITER

Steve originally trained and worked as a maths teacher before turning his hand to writing. His debut play **Damages** opened at The Bush Theatre in 2004 and went on to win the Meyer Whitworth Award in 2005. In 2006 his next play **Whipping It Up**, also premiered at The Bush Theatre before transferring to the New Ambassadors. **Whipping It Up** was later nominated for Best New Play in the Olivier Awards 2007 and Steve is currently adapting it as a comedy drama for Hartswood/BBC. He has also written a new TV drama **Parental Guidance** for BBC1 as well as writing for **Whistleblowers** (Carnival/ITV) and **Mutual Friends** (Hattrick/BBC). Steve is married to the barrister Lorna Skinner and they live in Hertfordshire and Cornwall with their three children.

painesPLOUGH

PAINES PLOUGH is an award-winning, nationally and internationally renowned theatre company, specialising exclusively in commissioning and producing new plays.

'…THE EVER-INVENTIVE PAINES PLOUGH…' The Independent

Paines Plough celebrates the writer's place at the heart of theatre, working with playwrights at every stage of their careers. We encourage and develop the very best emerging talent, as well as working with some of the most established names in theatre.

We think that great writing is the key to great theatre. We seek voices and stories that are as yet unheard, that have a special resonance or that speak to us in a unique way. Inspired by the creativity of our writers, we seek the most exciting spaces in which to produce our work. Recent productions have been seen in the nave of Canterbury Cathedral, a warehouse in Shoreditch, underground in Glasgow and late at night in the depths of London's West End.

We continue to seek partners with whom we can collaborate in a bold, responsive spirit to generate new plays that engage with the contemporary world.

'…PAINES PLOUGH'S NOMADIC THEATRE COMPANY HAS RACKED UP SO MANY STARS THAT BROWSING ITS PRESS RELEASE IS A BIT LIKE LOOKING INTO DEEP SPACE.' Metro

PAINES PLOUGH IS:
Artistic Director **Roxana Silbert**
General Manager **Anneliese Davidsen**
Literary Director **Tessa Walker**
Administrative Assistant **Livvy Morris**
Book-Keeper **Wojtek Trzcinski**
Senior Reader **Jane Fallowfield**
Pearson Playwright **Duncan Macmillan**

Board of Directors: Ola Animashawun, Tamara Cizeika, David Edwards, Chris Elwell, Fraser Grant, Marilyn Imrie, Clare O'Brien, Jenny Sealey

To find out more or to join our mailing list visit **www.painesplough.com**

Paines Plough is supported by Arts Council, England
Paines Plough has the support of the Pearson Playwrights' scheme
sponsored by Pearson plc and of Channel 4 for **Future Perfect**.

PERFORMANCE PROVOCATIVE AND COMPELLING THEATRE, COMEDY AND CABARET **TALKS** VIBRANT DEBATES ON CULTURE, THE ARTS AND THE WAY WE LIVE **SOHO CONNECT** A THRIVING EDUCATION, COMMUNITY AND OUTREACH PROGRAMME **WRITERS' CENTRE** DISCOVERING AND NURTURING NEW WRITERS AND ARTISTS **SOHO THEATRE BAR** SERVING TASTY, AFFORDABLE FOOD AND DRINK FROM 12PM TILL LATE.

'The capital's centre for daring international drama.'
EVENING STANDARD

'A jewel in the West End' BBC LONDON

THE TERRACE BAR
Drinks can be taken into the auditorium and are available from the Terrace Bar on the second floor.

SOHO THEATRE ONLINE
Giving you the latest information and previews of upcoming shows, Soho Theatre can be found on facebook, myspace and youtube as well as at sohotheatre.com

EMAIL INFORMATION LIST
For regular programme updates and offers visit sohotheatre.com/mailing

HIRING THE THEATRE
Soho Theatre has a range of rooms and spaces for hire. Please contact the theatre on 020 7287 5060 or go to sohotheatre.com/hires for further details.

Soho Theatre is supported by
ACE, Bloomberg, TEQUILA\London, Westminster City Council, The City Bridge Trust

Performances in the Lorenz Auditorium / Registered Charity No: 267234

SOHO STAFF

Artistic Director:
Lisa Goldman
Executive Director:
Mark Godfrey (sabbatical)
Acting Executive Director:
Catherine Thornborrow

BOARD OF DIRECTORS
Nicholas Allott (chair)
Sue Robertson (vice chair)
David Aukin
Norma Heyman
Jeremy King
Neil Mendoza
Simon Minty
Michael Naughton
David Pelham
Roger Wingate
Christopher Yu

HONORARY PATRONS
Bob Hoskins (President)
Peter Brook CBE
Simon Callow
Gurinder Chadha
Sir Richard Eyre CBE

ARTISTIC TEAM
Writers' Centre Director:
Nina Steiger
Soho Connect Director:
Suzanne Gorman
Producer – Late Night Programme:
Steve Lock
Casting Director: **Nadine Rennie**
International Associate: **Paul Sirett**
Artistic Associate: **Esther Richardson**
Director of Talks: **Palash Davé**
Writers' Centre Assistant:
Sheena Bucktowonsing
Soho Connect Workshop Leader:
Don McCamphill
Senior Reader: **Dale Heinan**

ADMINISTRATION
Acting General Manager:
Erin Gavaghan
Financial Controller: **Kevin Dunn**
Finance Officer: **Kate Wickens**
PA to Directors: **Amanda Joy**

MARKETING, DEVELOPMENT
AND PRESS
Marketing and Development Directors:
Elizabeth Duducu and **Jacqui Gellman**
Acting Head of Development: **Zoe Crick**
Marketing Manager: **Nicki Marsh**
Press and Public Relations:
Fiona McCurdy (020 7478 0142)
Development Assistant:
Zebina Nelson-Myrie
Marketing and New Media Assistant:
Alex Fleming
Access Officer: **Charlie Swinbourne**

BOX OFFICE AND FRONT OF HOUSE
Front of House and Events Manager:
Jennifer Dromey
Box Office Supervisor:
Natalie Worrall
Box Office Assistants:
**Danielle Baker, Lou Beere, Philip Elvy,
Tamsin Flessey, Lynne Forbes, Louise
Green, Eniola Jaiyeoba, Helen
Matthews, Leah Read, Becca Savory,
Traci Leigh Scarlett, Nida Vohra,**
and **Tom Webb.**
Duty Managers: **Colin Goodwin,
Martin Murphy.**
Front of House staff: **Carla Almeida,
Beth Aynsley, Thylda Bares, Adrian
Fubara, Louise Hall, Obi Iwumene,
Kyle Jenkins, Bea Kempton, Tony
Dinh Le, Matthew Lewis, Mutana
Mohmed, James Munroe, Kate
Mulley, Monique Sterling** and
Gemma Strong.

PRODUCTION
Production Manager: **Matt Noddings**
Technical Manager: **Nick Blount**
Head of Lighting: **Christoph Wagner**
Technician: **Natalie Smith**

**21 Dean Street,
London W1D 3NE
sohotheatre.com
Admin: 020 7287 5060
Box Office: 020 7478 0100**

THE SOHO THEATRE DEVELOPMENT CAMPAIGN

Soho Theatre receives core funding from Arts Council England, London. In order to provide as diverse a programme as possible and expand our audience development and outreach work, we rely upon additional support from trusts, foundations, individuals and businesses. All of our major sponsors share a common commitment to developing new areas of activity and encouraging creative partnerships between business and the arts. We are immensely grateful for the invaluable support from our sponsors and donors and wish to thank them for their continued commitment.

Soho Theatre has a Friends Scheme in support of its education programme and work developing new writers and reaching new audiences.

To find out how to become a Friend of Soho Theatre, contact the development department on **020 7478 0143**, or visit **sohotheatre.com**.

WINNER OF THE VERITY BARGATE AWARD 2007

this isn't romance

By In-Sook Chappell   Directed by Lisa Goldman
Design **Jon Bausor** Lighting **Jenny Kagan** Sound **Matt McKenzie**
With Sonnie Brown, Jennifer Lim (US), Elizabeth Tan and Mo Zainal

Identity, sex, twisted revenge. An Anglo-Korean model returns
to Seoul to find the brother she abandoned when adopted as a child.
A beautiful and brutal love story, this is the first play by British-Korean
writer **In-Sook Chappell**, winner of the **Verity Bargate Award 2007**.

12 February – 7 March 7.30pm

ROARING TRADE

Steve Thompson

*For my dad, who worked in Liverpool Street,
and for my mum, who made his dinner*

Characters

DONNY, *thirties, male, a bond trader*
JESS, *twenties, female, a bond trader*
PJ, *forties, male, a bond trader*
SPOON, *twenties, male, a bond trader*

SANDY, *forties, female, PJ's wife*
SEAN, *ten, male, Donny's son*

VOICES *of brokers and salespeople, unseen*

Staging Note

*The play takes place in many different locations, but multiple
sets are not required. Four chairs and four desks can be moved
around to create the different scenes.*

*Each trader has an upright microphone on his desk in order to
communicate with salespeople. The responses come out of a
small speaker situated at the base of the mic – a 'squawk box'.*

Author's Note

*A lot of people gave up their time to teach me the workings of
the City – thanks to all of them. Most of all I want to thank my
guide and guru, David Thompson. David is living proof that you
can work in the money markets and still be an unfailingly warm
and generous person.*

*This text went to press before the end of rehearsals and so may
differ slightly from the play as performed.*

ACT ONE

Scene One

Bond floor of a London investment bank – McSorley's.

2055hrs.

A window at the back reveals a panoramic sky at dusk: the spires of the City.

Trading is over for the day. The room is dark, except for the light from a desk lamp. A job interview is in progress. JESS, *the interviewer, is immaculate in a black suit and cream blouse. She speaks with a commanding dryness. The candidate is* DONNY. *He is tanned and good-looking, in a blue chalk pinstripe. His accent suggests East End London.*

She sits, he stands.

JESS. So. Donny McDaid. You're looking for a job? (*Breath.*)

DONNY. I brought my CV. (*Offers it.*)

JESS (*refusing to take it*). I know what it says.

DONNY. What?

JESS. I've seen nine guys already today. I know the resumé. Ten years in investment banking.

DONNY. Twelve. I did the Vodafone issue. And KCOM.

JESS. Who hates you?

DONNY. What?

Silence.

JESS. I do have to warn you, Donny, my boredom threshold is very low. This low. (*Indicates a minute fraction with her fingers.*)

DONNY. 'Who hates me?'

JESS. I've given up going to the theatre 'cause I don't have the attention span. I went to see *Lord of the Rings*. Sixty quid a seat. Five minutes in and I was staring at my shoes. You have to fight to keep my attention.

DONNY. Oh…

JESS. Frodo came on – in his little furry feet – and I sized the poor fucker up in seconds: good-hearted but flawed. That was Frodo. Will overcome adversity and ultimately triumph. After the interval I stayed in the bar.

Beat.

DONNY. I didn't see it.

JESS. I'm giving you your allocation. I promised you five minutes to make your pitch.

DONNY (*points to the CV*). I did Vodafone…

JESS. Tell me about your last job, Donny. It ended in a train wreck. Wanna know how I know?

An uncomfortable pause.

That's a lovely suit you're wearing. Boateng?

He nods.

I love Boateng. You haven't worn it for a while, though. No one who can afford Ozwald Boateng buys one that doesn't fit. What happened in your last job?

DONNY. Nothing.

Beat. She checks her watch and starts to rise.

Something.

JESS. Yes?

DONNY. Two million sterling. A deal.

She sits again.

DONNY *shifts uncomfortably – this is difficult to say.*

We'd been drinking.

JESS. Ah. Right. You were drunk when you got on to the floor.

Beat.

DONNY (*reluctantly*). I cocked an order up.

JESS. Because you were wankered.

DONNY. They said 'sell' and I thought they said 'buy'.

JESS (*laughs cruelly*). Woah! Now you've caught my attention! Far more eloquent than a line on your CV. I've an image of you now – you're a screw-up.

DONNY. It was just one trade.

JESS. One is all it takes. One bad trade and now you're desperate to get a job. (*Leaning forward.*) How desperate?

DONNY. Well…

JESS. Can we just swap places? (*Breath.*)

DONNY. What?

JESS. I gave you five minutes and you did very little to captivate me. But I'll give you five minutes more if I stand there and you sit here. Okay?

Beat. Then he accedes and swaps with her – he sits and she stands.

Kind of feels more natural – looking down on you, when you're trying to win my favour.

DONNY. Shall I go on?

JESS. It's a power thing. Me standing, you sitting.

DONNY. Shall I go on?

JESS. Better still, you could crouch on the floor in front of me.

Beat. DONNY *laughs a little. She doesn't. He realises with horror that she is serious.*

Long pause.

I know what you're thinking. I do. You're sitting there trying to second-guess me. You figure this is a test. And you want to work out – what's the right answer? Do I tell her to go to hell? Or do I smile and park my arse on the carpet? (*Beat.*) Depends on what I'm testing, doesn't it?

DONNY (*tentatively*). Why do you want me on the floor?

JESS. I want a lapdog.

Pause.

This is McSorley's. Second-largest bank in the Square Mile. Half our traders break the million-pound barrier. Just how far are you prepared to go?

Pause. He sits on the floor at her feet.

Good for you. Kneeling, I think.

He kneels.

And with your hands up, like a proper doggie.

Beat. He doesn't move.

(*Whispering.*) Come on, you've started now. Might even get points for going the furthest.

He shifts uncomfortably and raises his paws.

Good. And with your jacket off, please.

DONNY. What?

JESS. 'What?' – you didn't hear, or 'what?' – you've got to be kidding? (*Beat.*) This is a raging bull market. I've got guys here earning more than they'll spend in their lifetimes. Jacket.

Pause. He takes off his jacket.

And shirt.

He undresses. She takes his shirt and lays it on the chair. He kneels there, stripped to the waist.

She puts the tie back on him, tightens it and holds it like a dog's lead.

Well now. Let's think about your skills set. What skills will you be bringing to my team? (*Firing like a machine gun.*) What's seven per cent of seven?

DONNY. Nought point four-nine.

JESS. One-five-two divided by eight?

DONNY. Nineteen. Er... Yes! Nineteen.

JESS. Gilts at five-twenty. EIB one hundred over. What's the yield on ten years with a seven-per-cent coupon? (*Beat.*) Well?

DONNY. I can't...

She yanks the lead sharply. It makes him choke. He falls on to his hands.

JESS. You think I'm gonna employ you – line your pocket – without taming your arse first? Wrong. You arrogant fuckers need someone who can squash you. (*Breath.*) Don't you?

DONNY. Yes.

JESS. Yes. You do. You *need* taming.

She pulls him to his feet. She takes a Filofax off her desk, opens it at today's date and lays it open on her palm.

My diary.

DONNY. Uh-huh.

JESS. My contacts. Should probably pop you in it.

DONNY. What?

JESS. Just think of the symbolism. An expression of loyalty. You place yourself in my Filofax.

DONNY. 'Place myself'?

She lays her hand just next to his groin – the Filofax open on it.

(*Long syllable.*) Ah. (*Breath.*) You want me to...

JESS. Yes. Just pop it there.

DONNY. 'Pop'?

JESS. Lay it. Plonk it. Tells me what I need to know.

Beat.

DONNY. You promise you won't slam it shut?

JESS. Well now, Donny, isn't that the point of the exercise?

A very long pause.

DONNY. I really would like to work here.

JESS. It's a good place. They bake their own rolls downstairs in the café. (*Breath.*) Fresh panini. Beautiful flapjack.

DONNY. I like flapjack.

JESS. You've not lived until you've tried the one with cherries in.

He undoes his trousers. Pause.

Well?

DONNY. You do have a pension scheme? I mean, before I join, I just want to be clear about benefits.

JESS. Absolutely. A pension scheme. Stock options. And lovely cherry flapjack.

DONNY. Definitely the job for me, then.

He pulls open the front of his underwear. She reaches in.

PJ enters suddenly and switches on another desk lamp. Everyone freezes. PJ wears a suit and tie stained with beer. He is very drunk – even walking seems to present him with some difficulties.

PJ. I need to get to my desk. (*Breath.*) I need to get to my desk.

JESS *abruptly takes her hand out of* DONNY*'s pants.*

I'm sorry. If I'd known you were…

DONNY. Being interviewed.

PJ. Right.

PJ *rummages on his desk and finds his Oyster card whilst* JESS *turns her back and tries to compose herself.*

Pub's heaving. Wall to wall. Someone on the Japanese desk just made a bucketload.

He digs in his pocket and produces an iPod. He grins like a child.

Got an MP3 player. Japs were dishing 'em out.

JESS (*quietly, to* DONNY). Can we, perhaps, get him out of here?

PJ (*oblivious*). My youngest has got no excuse.

DONNY. What?

PJ. Not to cuddle me. MP3 for a cuddle.

JESS. Can we…? Please.

DONNY. You're buying her affection with that?

PJ. I'm not proud.

DONNY. No. Apparently.

JESS. Please do get into a conversation.

PJ *drops the iPod and it clatters to the floor. Beat. He retrieves it from the floor and strokes it as if it will help it to mend. He heads for the door and then turns.*

PJ. Donny?

DONNY. What?

PJ. Awesome day today. (*To* JESS.) The man has Lady Luck cupping his balls.

JESS. Fuck off, PJ.

PJ. Right.

PJ nods and exits. JESS and DONNY stare at one another. Beat. When they speak it is as if they are new characters – no longer in role.

JESS. Shit.

DONNY. It's fine.

JESS. Shit.

DONNY. It's fine.

JESS. Will he remember? (*Losing it.*) I would prefer this didn't make it round the whole team.

DONNY laughs gently.

Laugh all you want there, pal, but I'm not here for the quality of your roleplay. I want Asia-Pacific. You promised. I want that hedge fund. You're supposed to put in a word.

DONNY. I have. I will. I have. PJ won't remember shit. Don't start going all coy.

Pause. They hover awkwardly.

Look. Do you want to carry on or what?

Beat.

JESS. Can we just sprint to the finish? Do you mind?

DONNY. No. Absolutely.

She goes over to a desk, pushes the files to one side and sits on it. She starts to remove her underwear.

Scene Two

Trading, excerpt.

1110hrs.

The trading floor is in full swing.

Three desks side by side in spotlights: PJ, DONNY *and* JESS. *They are talking into their microphones and hearing replies through their squawk boxes.*

JESS *is busy and purposeful. She taps her computer keyboard whilst schmoozing the salespeople, reading the online bulletins and sugaring her coffee: a highly skilled multitasker.*

PJ *tries to be affable and relaxed – always the gentleman – even when he is down on the market. He focuses all of his attention on the caller.*

DONNY *is a curious cocktail of ebullience and laziness – he swings on his chair and flicks elastic bands in the air, whilst shouting louder than anyone else in the room.*

JESS. BT. Eight and a quarter. Four million. Yep?

VOICE 1 (*squawk, male, to* JESS). Market's one-oh-six.

PJ. Some Swiss. Will you take them off my plate?

VOICE 2 (*squawk, female, to* PJ). Read the bulletins. Swiss are in freefall.

DONNY. Bruno!

VOICE 2. Can't lift it. Nope.

JESS. Offer one-oh-seven, then.

VOICE 3 (*squawk, male, to* DONNY). Donnster!

VOICE 1. Hold, please.

DONNY. Turned the telly on last night. ITV3.

VOICE 3. Yeah?

DONNY. *Inspector* fucking *Morse*. All repeats.

PJ. Sell at one-two-seven?

VOICE 2. Not to me you won't.

VOICE 3. You like *Inspector Morse*?

DONNY. No, I fucking loathe it.

PJ. Listen, sweet…

DONNY. Comfy little dinner-time murders by middle-class academics.

PJ. I reckon I owe you a treat.

DONNY. Was already shit fifteen years ago.

VOICE 3. I guess you're not calling me up to buy ITV.

PJ. You and me in the box at Sandown.

VOICE 2. I'm not taking Swiss. They're in the cunt book, PJ. (*Hangs up.*)

VOICE 1. Jessica?

DONNY. I'm selling off my ITV.

VOICE 1. Jess?

DONNY. Bloody *Morse*. The one with Simon Callow.

VOICE 3. I hate that one.

   PJ *is dialling another number on his squawk box.*

JESS. One-oh-seven here.

VOICE 1. Wider than my granny's flaps.

DONNY. Selling all I've got. Fucking ITV is for pikeys.

VOICE 1. One-oh-six is my best price. I'm sorry.

JESS. Any bugger can be sorry.

DONNY. Two million.

VOICE 1. You're gonna go all sulky?

JESS. Biggest bull market this year. You should see the cars queuing up outside my Sainsbury's.

VOICE 4 (*squawk, male, to* PJ). Stan.

PJ. Hey. It's PJ here.

VOICE 4. Fuck off. I'm not interested.

JESS. And I was just starting to waver on coming for that drink.

PJ. Well, that's a fine 'good morning'.

VOICE 1. Hold on.

VOICE 3. Is this an order from your fund?

DONNY. Uh-huh. And they know how to be grateful.

PJ. I haven't told you what I'm after yet.

VOICE 4. I've read all the stuff online. You want out of Swiss Telecom.

VOICE 3. You're gonna make a cool half-million.

DONNY. Thanks. I've done the maths. I know the ins and outs of my arsehole.

PJ. My risk limit's close.

VOICE 4. You're long and wrong, pal.

VOICE 3. I'm liking this.

DONNY. Clean the fucking deal up and close it down.

PJ. Please.

VOICE 4. Don't beg me. Begging isn't nice. (*Hangs up.*)

PJ (*to the room*). I've got twelve million Swiss collapsing. I'm losing thousands.

    JESS *hears him and turns.*

DONNY (*hangs up. Punches the air victoriously*). You know why we have glass walls? It's so everyone can admire me.

PJ (*rubs his face and stares at the screen*). Just sitting here, bleeding.

DONNY *leaps up and takes a bow to an imaginary crowd of admirers.* JESS *taps the keys of her keyboard.* PJ *stares at his screen, hopeless.*

Everyone's squawk boxes are already buzzing for the next call.

Scene Three

Bond floor.

1343hrs.

SPOON *stands alone. He is an attractive, ruddy-faced public schoolboy.*

Beside him on the floor is a cardboard carton with some personal items. He's moving in.

DONNY *enters briskly. He carries a Styrofoam cup of coffee, a bottle of water and some chocolate bars.*

DONNY. What are you?

SPOON. Sorry? What?

DONNY. What *are* you?

SPOON (*extends his hand*). Ollie.

DONNY. I asked, 'what'.

SPOON. I'm an employee.

DONNY. Of?

SPOON. I work *here*.

DONNY. You empty the bins?

Beat.

SPOON. I'm new.

DONNY. You from the Black Hole of Calcutta?

SPOON. I don't get...

DONNY. The graduate office. No windows, so they say. (*Breath.*) Must feel like a different world up here. Sexy secretaries. Lovely thick carpets. Clean air. Are you on an errand or something?

SPOON. They phoned. They said a desk had... opened up.

DONNY. Ah. Right.

For the first time, DONNY *stops in his tracks and looks* SPOON *up and down.*

SPOON. I've been here half an hour.

DONNY (*dry, quiet*). Makes you the longest-serving graduate we've ever had. Congratulations.

SPOON. I didn't get your name.

DONNY. One cunt wouldn't get out the elevator. Went up and down all day, trying to summon up the bottle. I mean, a man could start to feel offended – the number of new guys who've walked out on us. Thanks for sticking at it.

SPOON. I didn't get...

DONNY. Very nice suit you're wearing. (*Breath.*) I like suits. I am a connoisseur. A suitist.

SPOON. Er...

DONNY (*ignoring him*). Pink's shirt?

SPOON. Yes...

DONNY. Tie – Hermès?

SPOON. Yes.

DONNY. And cufflinks? I can't quite see them…

SPOON. Jesus, Cambridge.

DONNY. Oh. You're Spoony. (*Breath*.)

SPOON. What?

DONNY. 'Silver Spoon.' Born with. In your trap.

SPOON (*confused*). I got a First.

DONNY. In being Spoony?

SPOON. Physics, actually.

DONNY. Woo-hooh. What were you – a rugby blue?

SPOON. Rowing.

DONNY. Rowing – phoo! We've not had one of you cunts for a
while.

In the silence that follows, SPOON *peruses the vacant desk.
The previous incumbent has left a few items.* DONNY *eats
his lunch all the while – dunking a Kit Kat into his coffee
and sucking off the warm chocolate.*

SPOON. Who was *he*?

DONNY. Who was who?

SPOON. My… predecessor.

There is a stapler with a name scratched on the side.

(*Reads*.) 'Alf.'

DONNY. That wasn't his name. We just called him that.

SPOON. 'Alf'?

DONNY. A.L.F. Aggressive – little – fucker.

SPOON. Ah. Right.

DONNY. Had all the hedge funds tucked in his pocket. Spotted
what he thought was a good deal. Went for a mid-morning
poo – it had turned into a cuntfest. Visiting the toilet is folly,

Ollie. The world can turn on its head before you've taken your pants down.

SPOON *finishes his unpacking. He is hovering over the chair, about to sit.* DONNY *points at him and barks.*

Er... sorry. You don't get his chair.

SPOON. What?

DONNY. Not until you've put your time in.

SPOON. So, where will I be?

DONNY. You'll be lurking. You will develop your 'lurk'. 'Can have a desk but not a chair. A chair is being fucking cheeky.' (*Breath.*) I've seen men slave for years before they've been allowed a chair. Be on your pins most of the day... Getting sandwiches; visiting the vendor; and if we need a shoeshine – that's also your domain.

SPOON. Look...

DONNY (*reaches down into his desk drawer*). If anyone has dry-cleaning they'll probably ask you to pop it over the road. (*He produces a can of polish and a duster from his desk.*) Most days you'll need to run round with the duster.

SPOON. You've got to be kidding me.

DONNY. You don't look all that thrilled.

Silence.

SPOON (*almost speechless – fighting for words*). I went to Cambridge. I've got a First.

DONNY. All of us were the brightest in our year. Waltzed in here, strutting like ponies. The cleaner's got a doctorate.

SPOON. Look...

DONNY. Ten a penny round here. Used to be: you got a job if you could just stand up straight and spell your name. Now it's all, 'What did you do *your* PhD in?' We're all prodigies. And you were the last to arrive. So.

He hands the can of polish and the duster to SPOON *and nods for him to begin.* SPOON *doesn't move.* DONNY *points at a spot on his desk that needs a polish.*

JESS *enters suddenly. She carries an expensive handbag. She swans straight past* SPOON, *who is carrying his can of polish and his duster.*

(*To* JESS.) And she's back. Well, what did you have then?

JESS. I had the garganelli.

DONNY. Good call. Garganelli with chard. Did you have it with the peas or the asparagus?

JESS. I had peas. Puréed.

DONNY. Fucking 'puréed'. Listen to you.

JESS. Not on the menu, but I spoke to the waiter.

DONNY. Fucking pea purée! And to follow?

JESS. We had fondant. (*Breath.*)

DONNY. 'We'?

JESS. Two spoons.

DONNY. You shared dessert?

JESS. Our spoons were gently touching.

DONNY. You shared dessert with the client!?

JESS. Placed an order.

DONNY (*amused; delighted*). I'll fucking bet he did.

JESS. Five million.

DONNY. You. Two fucking spoons!

JESS. Wiped the chocolate off his mouth and signed up.

DONNY. I wish I had bosoms.

She shrugs and begins work.

I've got to do a whole weekend of serious grovelling just to get an order like that. Getting them pissed – getting them laid.

JESS. Love bombing.

DONNY. Yeah. A whole festival of champagne and lap-dancing. You – you just wiggle your dugs and he pays up.

PJ returns from lunch, looking pink.

PJ. Tally-ho.

They all ignore him.

JESS. It's much more than just a wiggle, my friend.

DONNY. Yeah? Is it?

JESS. It's the promise attached to the wiggle. The gentle 'come hither' that always remains unspoken.

DONNY. The sense that you might take him to the toilet and gobble him off after pudding.

JESS. Yeah. In a nutshell.

PJ (*to the whole room*). Tell me, tell me, my children – how do we feel about butter curls?

DONNY and JESS sigh audibly and turn to their computer screens to begin work.

DONNY. Oh, here we go.

PJ. Do they still warrant a place on the restaurant table?

DONNY. Have you had a whole bottle to yourself?

PJ. I am instigating a lively discussion about which dairy spreads we all favour.

They all ignore him and carry on working. Pause.

I, myself, am very taken by the spreads that combine veg-etable oils with buttermilk. The benefit being that they taste like butter but still remain soft. Even after refrigeration.

Beat. Still no response.

Jess?

JESS. Do I really have to answer?

PJ. Are you struggling to form an opinion?

JESS. I'm struggling to ignore you.

DONNY. She has the same rule as me: never to debate you
when you're just back from lunch.

Silence.

PJ. And is this a view shared by everyone?

JESS. Yesterday, PJ, you had us debating 'town planning'.

DONNY (*not looking up*). 'Is the supermarket destroying the
corner shop?'

JESS. 'Is the supermarket destroying the corner shop?'

PJ. What did we decide?

JESS. On Tuesday we had a lengthy 'set-to' about George
Formby.

DONNY. 'Was he even talented?'

JESS. It's not that we don't adore you, PJ. But you've worn us
down, that's all.

DONNY. No remaining capacity for small talk.

PJ (*vibrant for the first time*). It isn't small.

JESS. PJ...

PJ. It isn't small! There's a world out there and I want us to
embrace it. We spend eleven hours a day in here, staring at
Bloomberg. Even battery hens peck each other.

PJ *notices* SPOON *for the first time.*

Starting today?

SPOON. Mm.

PJ. Really? (*He points at the suit.*) Kenzo?

DONNY. Paul Smith.

PJ. Oh? (*Points at the shirt.*) Pink's?

> SPOON *nods.*

> Hermès?

> SPOON *nods again.*

> Cufflinks?

DONNY. Jesus, Cambridge.

PJ (*nods, impressed*). I see he's got you with his polish and duster.

SPOON. What?

PJ (*grins*). Did he say you have to shine our shoes?

> SPOON *realises he has been had. He looks sharply at*
> DONNY. DONNY *grins.*

DONNY. You're gonna be great fun.

> SPOON *throws down the can and the duster.* DONNY
> *laughs cruelly.*

Scene Four

Fast-food restaurant.

1825hrs.

A table with two chairs. DONNY *sits opposite his ten-year-old son,* SEAN.

They have burgers and fries in front of them, in cardboard containers and plates. SEAN *has acquired a free toy with the meal – an action figure.* DONNY *is working on his laptop, staring at the screen.*

SEAN. You have to look.

> DONNY *obliges and looks up from his work.* SEAN *clenches his fist in a tight ball and holds it out to* DONNY *with the thumb at the top.*

Lift the lid.

> DONNY *obliges, lifting up his son's thumb.*

Now put your finger in.

> DONNY *puts his finger in the hole made by his son's clenched fingers.*

Stir it round.

> DONNY *wiggles his finger.*

Thanks for cleaning my toilet.

> SEAN *collapses in hysterics at this joke.* DONNY *is unmoved. He returns to his work.*

Isn't it brilliant?

DONNY (*expressionless*). It is. It's brilliant.

SEAN. It's so funny.

DONNY. It's on a par with the comic greats.

> *Beat.*

SEAN. He did it in the library corner.

DONNY. And you laughed?

> SEAN *nods.*

And that's why the teacher did her nut.

SEAN. No.

DONNY. No?

> *Beat.* SEAN *is reluctant to elaborate.*

SEAN. I was doing armpit farts. (*Breath.*) Dylan dared me to do it. Mrs Bayliss saw.

DONNY. Ah. (*Breath.*)

SEAN. You're supposed to tell me off. Mum wants you to tell me off.

DONNY. For armpit farts? She's concerned.

Beat. DONNY *is engaged with his work.*

SEAN. Tell me off.

DONNY (*unenthusiastically*). You're scum.

SEAN. No, properly.

DONNY. 'Properly'?

SEAN. I'm 'a troublemaker'.

DONNY. Your mother's sent you here with a script?

SEAN *nods again.* DONNY *looks up.*

I ate a worm once.

SEAN (*eyes light up*). You're kidding.

DONNY. At school. One bite. Not the whole worm.

SEAN. What'd it taste like, then?

DONNY. Gorgeous. (*Breath.*) Somebody dared me, Sean. *I* got called a troublemaker too.

SEAN. This is why we're having tea. You're supposed to be 'having a word'.

DONNY (*to himself again*). Of course. She won't let me take you abroad, but if she thinks you need telling off, suddenly I get open access.

SEAN. Dad…

DONNY (*looking straight at* SEAN). What your mum hasn't grasped here, Sean – we don't have the same definition of 'the word'. (*Breath.*)

SEAN. What word?

DONNY. 'Trouble.' I don't run from trouble. And neither should you. Trouble means that the world is afraid.

SEAN. Er…

DONNY (*leans forward, as if sharing a secret*). And when people are afraid – you exploit it.

SEAN (*confused, after a breath*). You're not saying 'stay out of trouble'.

DONNY. God, no. I made seventy million quid after the war in Iraq. 'Buy on the sound of guns.'

SEAN. Er…

DONNY. Trouble is an opportunity. If Dylan wanted armpit farts you should have charged him.

SEAN *is confused*.

SEAN. Mrs Bayliss said…

DONNY. They give us a limit. How much you can gamble. A 'risk limit', it's called. Eight million pounds, your dad. You think Mrs Bayliss would ever gamble eight million sterling? Trouble gets you places. Trouble is why your dad drives around in a Lexus. Have I told you how to 'short' yet?

SEAN *looks blank*.

No?

SEAN. You told me what a bond is. It's like an IOU or something.

DONNY *gestures for him to elaborate*.

Coca-Cola needs to make money… they sell bonds to people.

DONNY. Which are?

SEAN (*finding trouble with the definition*). Bits of paper… promising money.

DONNY. Precious bits of paper that tell the whole world you made Coca-Cola a loan. And these IOUs – these bonds – they get bought and sold. It's called…

SEAN. 'Buying debt.'

DONNY. 'Buying debt.' Good lad. You've got this IOU – and you sell it to another bloke. For cash. That's all that's happening.

SEAN (*trying to understand*). Er… So – he's got *your* IOU.

DONNY. Yes.

SEAN. He paid you for it.

DONNY. Yes.

SEAN. And then… Coke pay *him* back, instead.

DONNY (*nods*). It's the money-go-round, my sweetpea. Ownership of debt. What your old dad does for a living. (*Beat. Eats.*)

SEAN. Mum says it's just like selling veg off a barrow.

DONNY. Balls. It's much more skilled.

SEAN. 'Like selling veg.'

DONNY. Actually says that, does she?

SEAN *nods*.

(*To himself, under his breath.*) Veg wouldn't pay off her car loan. (*To* SEAN.) Where was I?

SEAN (*prompting*). Shorting.

Suddenly DONNY *is animated. He reaches on to the side of his plate and takes the unopened sachet of ketchup.*

DONNY. The price of this ketchup is falling, Sean. What do you do?

SEAN. Er…

DONNY. Can't do nothing. Sell it, Sean. Sell the ketchup.

SEAN. It's yours. I've had my ketchup.

DONNY. Doesn't matter. Doesn't matter that it isn't yours. (*Wielding the ketchup sachet.*)You can still make money off it.

SEAN. I don't get you.

DONNY (*points to the action figure on the table*). The man you're selling it to – he doesn't know that the ketchup isn't even yours. He won't collect it from you 'til the end of the day. Sell it to him. Take his money. Now.

SEAN. I'm confused.

DONNY. Sell it to him. Ten pee.

SEAN. But…

DONNY *silences him with a raised hand. He digs his wallet out and hands his son a ten-pence piece.*

DONNY. You just earned your commission on this ketchup, Seanie.

SEAN. I'm getting money for selling *your* ketchup?

DONNY. See how good it feels. Selling something you don't even own.

SEAN. But…

DONNY. The ketchup market is in a very bad way. The price has started spiralling down. At the end of the day the price of ketchup has fallen to five pee. Half of what it was. So *that's* when you buy it from me. (*Hands it to him.*)

SEAN. At the end of the day?

DONNY. When the price of ketchup has fallen. Sell it when it costs a lot… *then* buy it when the price falls.

SEAN. And then give it to the bloke?

DONNY. Yes. (*Gives it to the action figure.*) Isn't that smart?

SEAN. Woah. Yeah.

DONNY. Don't have to run off in tears 'cause the market's in a slump. You *use* the situation, Sean. You *use* the fact that ketchup prices are falling.

SEAN. You want it to fall.

DONNY. So you can exploit it. Yes.

SEAN. Can you make it go down if you want?

DONNY. What?

SEAN. Can you make the price go down?

DONNY. How?

SEAN. Tell everyone that ketchup tastes like dog poo.

DONNY (*smiles; proud*). Smart.

SEAN. Tell everyone. Make the price fall.

DONNY. Sadly – against the rules. Or everyone would do it.

SEAN *nods eagerly – finally he understands the concept. He tucks into his dinner.*

(*Still admiring.*) Dylan's gonna end up working for *you*, Sean. Tell yourself you're better than he is. Say it to him.

Silence. SEAN *finishes eating and stares at* DONNY. *He pushes his plate away.*

Are you not eating those? Pass them over here.

As DONNY *reaches for the cardboard plate,* SEAN *pulls it away.*

SEAN. No.

DONNY. What?

SEAN. Make me an offer.

DONNY *stares at his son, surprised.*

DONNY. Take your hand off that plate.

SEAN. No.

DONNY. Sean, I'm your dad.

SEAN. I know. And you're still hungry. (*Breath.*)

DONNY smiles a little.

DONNY. I could buy more.

SEAN. I'll price these lower.

Silent stand-off.

DONNY. Okay. Now I'm gonna beat the crap out of you.

SEAN relinquishes his grasp on the chips.

No. Don't let go. If I'm angry – that means they're worth a great deal.

Beat. SEAN picks up his carton of chips again.

Scene Five

Trading, excerpt.

0925hrs.

Four desks side by side in spotlights: PJ, DONNY, SPOON *and* JESS.

DONNY. One-oh-three – got a very clean arse.

VOICE 5 (*squawk, male, to* DONNY). One-oh-one?

DONNY. That's not an offer, that's a fucking embarrassment.

JESS. Will you give me a price for three million?

VOICE 6 (*squawk, male, to* SPOON). What you got?

SPOON (*reading the internet bulletins*). Er… I've got BT at six and three-quarters.

VOICE 6. Doesn't give me a chubby in my shorts.

VOICE 5. Try for one-oh-two.

SPOON. Let me see what else is here.

VOICE 7 (*squawk, male, to* JESS). One hundred.

DONNY (*to* SPOON). Say MediaCorp.

SPOON (*to* DONNY). What?

PJ. Twenty million.

DONNY. Everyone is buying it, Spoon. You tell him.

VOICE 8 (*squawk, female, to* PJ). Can't shift it.

PJ. Then don't tell him twenty. Say five.

DONNY (*to* SPOON). I'm all over it. Seriously.

VOICE 5. One-oh-two. Yeah?

SPOON (*to client*). Try MediaCorp?

VOICE 8. I can't shift it.

SPOON (*to* JESS). Did you hear him? Helping me.

JESS (*to* SPOON). I know. Isn't he a peach?

DONNY (*to* SPOON). Don't waste your time scouring the internet – bulletin boards can be dodgy.

JESS. Gee, thanks, Pop.

VOICE 6. Two million.

SPOON *smiles at* DONNY *– full of gratitude – and writes it into his book.*

VOICE 5. One-oh-two.

SPOON. That's done for you.

VOICE 5. Do you still want to buy?

DONNY. I've done my trades, pal, whilst you were sitting there scratching. (*Breath.*) Be first, be right and be quiet.

DONNY *hangs up. He is immediately dialling another number.* SPOON *is eagerly writing his order on to his computer.*

SPOON (*to* DONNY). Did *you* buy some as well?

DONNY (*to* SPOON). I don't want to buy, I want to sell.

Pause. SPOON *is confused.*

SPOON. You just said 'everyone is buying'.

DONNY. 'Cause I want to drive up the price. Thanks for helping, Jesus boy.

SPOON. What? You mean…?

PJ (*to himself*). Find me twenty million quid.

SPOON (*to* DONNY). You were shitting me?

DONNY (*to* SPOON). Oh, smack my bum. I don't give out sales advice. Sorry.

SPOON *stares at him but does not move.*

SPOON. You said 'buy'.

DONNY. Yes. We've mastered the concept. I wanted the price to go up.

PJ (*to* DONNY). You suck Satan's winkle.

SPOON. You got me to spend two million just to give you a better price?

DONNY. I made you my bitch, yeah.

For a moment SPOON *is dumbfounded – unable to find a response.*

SPOON. You bumbag!

DONNY (*laughs*). Ooh. Is that how they swear at Cambridge?

SPOON. Fucking bumbag.

DONNY (*amused*). Best fucking uni in the land. Except if you're there to learn swearing.

SPOON. I just spent two million of someone's money.

Beat. SPOON *looks around the room – JESS is grinning and* PJ *is shaking his head softly. They all know what has happened.*

(*To* JESS.) Did you know? Did you know what he was doing?

JESS *grins but won't look at him.*

PJ. School of hard knocks. Happens to us all.

SPOON. You could have said.

DONNY (*amused*). Not cricket?

SPOON. You could have told me – someone could.

PJ. 'Swhat we do.

DONNY. It's not against the law, you fucking prawn.

JESS (*without even looking round at him*). If you don't know who the fool is in the market...

PJ. Then the fool in the market...

DONNY. Is probably you!

He taps SPOON *on the nose.* SPOON *brushes his hand away angrily.* DONNY *laughs. He picks up a handful of* SPOON*'s order papers and lobs them in the air. They shower the room.*

SPOON. Hey!

SPOON tries unsuccessfully to catch them all before they get lost in the mess. The squawk boxes are ringing again.

Scene Six

Suburban dining room.

2032hrs.

The table is laid.

A dinner for one: a single dinner plate with a knife and fork, a single bread roll in a basket and a small cheeseboard.

SANDY *sits at the table reading some documents. She has already eaten. Her empty plate is in front of her – knife and fork pushed together.*

The front door opens and shuts offstage. Pause. PJ *enters, in his suit.*

SANDY. You stayed for a drink? (*Breath.*) I'm not checking up. You deserve a drink, Paul. (*Beat.*) I made a tuna lasagne.

PJ. Well.

SANDY. Top's a bit brown. But I'm sure it tastes, you know.

PJ. I'm sure.

Beat. SANDY *exits.* PJ *sits alone playing with his cutlery.*

After a moment she returns and plonks the earthenware dish on the table. PJ *looks at it.*

I left them in the pub. They're going on somewhere after.

SANDY. I imagine. (*Breath.*)

PJ. What are those bits? Lying on the top.

SANDY. Slices of egg. (*Remembering.*) Serving spoon. I'll go and get one.

She exits. He glances at her pile of documents and then shouts to her offstage.

PJ. What's all this, then?

SANDY (*offstage*). Budget.

PJ. What budget?

SANDY. For school. (*She reappears with the serving spoon.*)
What the Chair of Governors has to do these days.

PJ. Plan the budget?

SANDY. Library books; classrooms.

PJ. So… what do the teachers do?

SANDY. Teachers know sod all about funding.

She gives him the serving spoon and sits down to her documents again.

They want new gym apparatus. (*Breath.*) Nine thousand.

PJ. You could just write them a cheque.

SANDY (*smiles*). Not the point. I'm going to organise a fête.
Bake cakes.

PJ. Nine thousand pounds?

SANDY (*shrugs*). Just have to bake a lot. (*She studies his face.*)
What's up?

PJ. Nothing.

SANDY (*guesses correctly*). They gave you a date. For your
bonus.

PJ. Yes.

SANDY. And?

PJ. 'And'?

SANDY. Don't be annoying…

PJ. This Thursday?

He nods. She looks distantly pleased with this news.

SANDY. Like winning the lottery. Once a year.

PJ. Mm. Feels like playing the lottery, certainly.

Beat. She is reading again.

Can you imagine the build-up? Called in, one by one. The long, slow walk to the guillotine.

SANDY. I remember them. Every year. I always remember your bonus…

PJ (*finishing her thought*). …on account of the holidays.

SANDY (*nods*). After the Mirror merger we went to Barbados.

PJ. And when Russia ran dry we went to Bournemouth.

SANDY. It's been a good year. Money about.

PJ. That's not what they're saying to us.

SANDY. Really?

PJ. Clever sods. No. They spread the rumour for a week or so – not such a big profit as they'd hoped. Means when they offer us tuppence ha'penny we're all supposed to be pleasantly surprised. (*Breath.*)

SANDY. You'll have to do a face.

PJ. Pardon?

SANDY. 'Only four hundred grand.' (*She pulls a face.*) Practise looking… disappointed. (*Beat.*) If they think they might lose you to another bank – they'll soon start adding on the zeroes.

PJ (*shrugs; unconvinced*). You do the face when you come *out* of his office – clutching your bonus offer in your hand. There's no visibility, you see.

SANDY. You mean no one knows what everyone else is getting.

PJ. No. (*Eats.*) No one admits to a crappy bonus.

SANDY (*laughs a little*). Like admitting that your penis is unusually small. So… do a contented face. Make the guys think you've got something big in your pocket.

PJ. Then there's the risk you overdo it and everyone knows you're overcompensating. (*Eats.*) I've never been to a sauna, but I bet it's remarkably bloody similar. No one knows what's under your towel. All you can do is to look at the face. And guess.

SANDY. It's been a good year, Paul. And you're a good trader. Everyone's apprehensive.

Pause. She is reading. He stares at her.

PJ. The girls are both at uni.

SANDY. Sorry?

PJ. We've got savings. They'll be leaving home.

SANDY. I don't...

PJ. I was thinking about... a stop date.

Beat. She stares back.

SANDY. What?

PJ. I was...

SANDY. What?

PJ. I was...

SANDY. A 'stop date'?

PJ. You can't... for ever...

SANDY. A 'stop date'! You're thinking about... leaving?

PJ. Maybe this is the year. (*Breath.*) People don't... past their forties...

SANDY. This year?

PJ. I know. You want a new kitchen.

SANDY. Sod the kitchen. What about the girls?

PJ. They're both at uni.

SANDY. There are fees. They need a place to stay.

PJ. Sandy.

SANDY. Families cost money, Paul. You're not even old. (*Breath*.)

PJ. I am.

SANDY. You can't just… resign.

PJ. I *am* old. I am walking in that office to pick up my bonus offer. The guys before me – they all could be… my kids.

SANDY. Paul…

PJ. Blokes I trained. Come out with bigger smiles – better money. Don't you think that's just a bit humiliating?

SANDY. Of course. But not this year.

PJ. We've had three different sofas since we moved! Three brand new sets of lounge furniture. I've not had the chance to sit in any of them.

SANDY. Paul…

PJ. Sandy, I work fourteen-hour days and then sleep the whole weekend.

SANDY. Paul.

PJ. What's the point in seven sodding bedrooms? I never see this house in the daylight. I want some time.

SANDY. But not this year.

PJ. Look. Look…

SANDY. You've got another year surely.

PJ (*gentle laugh*). 'One more year', yeah? Stay for one more bonus. (*Silence*.) It's like a pact you have to make. Give your soul up now. Enjoy the rewards… maybe next year.

SANDY (*softly*). Listen to me…

PJ (*plays with the food on his fork*). I shift cash from one pile to another. Yesterday you were down. Today it's someone else's turn. It's not real – it's so fragile. It's nothing. Pretend games. Promises. Pushing IOUs around the room.

SANDY. Listen…

PJ. Some little tinpot bank wants to be the new leader – so it storms into the paper market.

SANDY. Yes…

PJ. Borrowing more than you can afford so you can lend it to someone who has no hope of paying you back. (*Looking straight at her.*) Nothing we do makes a difference to the way the world turns on its axis.

SANDY. It makes a difference to us. As a family. We need…

PJ (*scoffs*). Seven bedrooms.

SANDY. I still want the girls to have a room – when they come back and visit us! And we want to take them on holiday. God willing, we're going to have to pay for two splendid weddings. I don't want us all just… 'making do'. None of us. What's wrong with you? You have to be hungry to succeed. (*Breath. No answer.*) If it were me…

PJ. Yes.

SANDY. If I was still working at the bank…

PJ. Then you'd be buying *me* a kitchen. (*Breath.*)

SANDY. But I left. I was happy to leave. And now.

PJ. Yes. Okay. Let's start the evening again.

He tucks into his food.

Scene Seven

Train platform, Docklands Light Railway.

2210hrs.

SPOON *is standing on the platform. He has a copy of the evening newspaper. He looks slightly dishevelled after an evening spent drinking.*

JESS *arrives. She spots him and strolls over.*

JESS (*affable*). Hi.

He turns and sees her.

SPOON. Hi.

VOICE (*a muffled announcement over the loudspeaker system*). We apologise for the late running of the eight ten to Lewisham. This is due to a faulty door mechanism.

Pause.

JESS. 'Sgot to feel good.

SPOON. Sorry? What?

JESS. It's got to feel good. Today, Ollie.

He looks uncertain – she spells it out.

You had a good one.

SPOON. Mm. Cable & Wireless. You heard?

JESS. Yes.

SPOON. Five hundred grand, I made. Nearly.

JESS. I heard you talking. (*Breath.*) In the pub. I heard you talking in the pub.

SPOON. Kind of busy.

JESS. Mm. Heaving. I saw you, though – getting the beers in.

SPOON. They bought me champagne.

JESS. 'They'?

SPOON. To celebrate. Four hundred quid for a bottle.

JESS. Because you made your first half-million.

SPOON. Four hundred quid. They all chipped in.

JESS (*dry*). Wow.

SPOON. I'm sorry…

JESS. What?

SPOON. You didn't get some.

JESS. Yes. My heart *was* breaking.

SPOON. Felt good, though.

JESS. What?

SPOON. Today. Felt good.

JESS (*a wry smile*). You mean, making half a million? Or feeling them all pat you on the back?

Beat. They wait together. He has a sense that she is being distantly critical but he cannot see the reason.

SPOON. My dad was in the City.

JESS. I'll bet.

SPOON. He was on the board at Shads.

JESS. Well, no wonder you came over well at interview.

SPOON. He says relationships are… key.

JESS. Uh-huh.

SPOON. The pub-culture thing.

JESS. Uh-huh.

SPOON. Friday nights.

JESS. 'Gentlemanly capitalism.'

SPOON. He says the pub is a crucial place to be.

JESS. Yeah? (*Turns to him.*) So: what did you chat about?

SPOON. What?

JESS. Once they'd toasted your good fortune. (*Breath.*) You were talking. You and the lads. Presumably the banter moved on from 'congratulations'.

SPOON. Er… We were talking cars.

JESS (*amused*). Uh-huh. 'What are you driving these days?'

SPOON. Yes. Just being friendly. (*Half-breath.*) It's what colleagues do, isn't it?

JESS (*now laughing*). 'Colleagues.' Compete all day. And then buy each other beers and swap stories. (*As if sharing a secret.*) When you get into work tomorrow – sit in your chair. And then turn to your left and your right. One of those guys beside you will be gone within six months. There *are* no colleagues.

SPOON. Oh, come on…

JESS. No good turning thirty-million profit – not if the guy beside you makes forty. So they all get together at night and they size each other up. Compare cars; compare wives; compare homes.

SPOON. We were…

JESS. 'Your place in Wiltshire – how's it coming?' 'My dick is green, and twelve acres. Can I compare it to yours?'

SPOON. You really think that's why they go drinking?

JESS. It's a pissing contest. Bonus day is next week!

VOICE. Platform One for Lewisham.

Pause.

JESS (*leans in close*). Four hundred quid on champagne. You think that's a sign of their admiration? You had a good day. You need squashing. That champagne was to unnerve you.

VOICE. Platform One for Lewisham.

Pause. JESS *collects her things.*

JESS. How did they offer you this job?

SPOON. 'How'?

JESS. Phone call? Letter? Tied to a brick? How did you hear? (*Breath.*)

SPOON. I think *I* phoned *them*. (*Breath.*) Yes. Yes, *I* phoned *them*.

JESS. Two days after interview.

SPOON. Uh-huh. I spoke to... some PA.

JESS. And she offered you the job?

SPOON. Well, no.

JESS (*a big grin*). No. She didn't, did she?

SPOON. I mean, she didn't say... She *didn't* say that I *hadn't* got it. I just assumed.

JESS. They never offer. Not out loud. Don't want to give you the chance to say 'no'. They just wait for you to... assume. Just wait and see how arrogant you are. (*The sound of a train. She stands.*) There are two ways you can go. You can go up there and try to make a living. Or you can go in determined to be 'best'. But then he'll make you fight.

SPOON. Fight?

JESS (*sweetly*). Donny. Half a million. He'll have noticed.

And the train arrives.

Scene Eight

Trading, excerpt.

1535hrs.

Trading is in progress: this time it is just DONNY *and* SPOON *in spotlights.*

They are both tapping the keys of their computers – entering the sales data. DONNY *looks up and grins.*

DONNY. 'Fig Jam.' (*Breath.*) I'm gonna change my name. Have it done official. Get everyone to call me 'Fig Jam'.

SPOON. 'Fig Jam'?

DONNY. Yeah. What d'ya reckon? Catchy?

SPOON. I don't get it…

DONNY. 'Fuck-I'm-Good, Just-Ask-Me.'

SPOON. Ah.

DONNY. Five million. Since lunch.

He digs into a big bag of Minstrels on his desk. He stuffs a handful in his mouth and then lobs a few of them at SPOON.

Each new sentence – each boast – begins with a sweet being thrown at SPOON*'s head.*

(*Throw.*) Two million Konex, short since this morning. (*Throw.*) Another one-point-two short – BT. (*Throw.*) And now BSkyB – five more. (*Beat. Throw.*) I have just gambled eight million quid.

SPOON (*sarcastic*). Woah.

DONNY. You got the dick to do something like that, have you, Spoon?

SPOON is trying hard to ignore him – focussing on the details of his trading screen. But DONNY *wants a response so he strolls over.*

Teach you how to hold a cricket bat. Teach you a good sculling stroke. Can't teach you everything.

SPOON. I made nearly half a million yesterday.

DONNY. And I made eight by shorting the market. So.

DONNY *throws sweets again.* SPOON *turns.*

SPOON. What about a risk limit, Donny?

DONNY. What about it?

SPOON. Well… it matters.

DONNY. What they let you play?

SPOON. Four. I risk more than four million quid, I get a scolding.

DONNY. So? (*Leans in. Whispers.*) Step over the line a bit.

SPOON. Pardon?

DONNY. The serious people do it. The people who aren't frightened to try.

SPOON. 'Step over the line'?

DONNY. Not your nature? Worried about detention after school? Let's see you gamble all of it at once.

DONNY *starts to fiddle with* SPOON*'s keyboard – writing a massive order.* SPOON *pushes him away.*

SPOON. Hey.

DONNY. You need fucking concrete gonads – shorting the market – selling bonds that you don't even own. (*Numbering on his fingers.*) Five plus two plus one-point-two. Let me see you do better. Let's gamble all you've got, shall we?

Again, DONNY *reaches for the keyboard and* SPOON *pushes him away.*

SPOON. Your limit is what?

DONNY. Eight.

SPOON. Million?

DONNY. Yeah. Eight.

SPOON. So *you* went over? Burst your limit?

DONNY. Just a little. Risk and reward, Spoon, my friend. You want to shag one of them – her sister always wants to join in.

DONNY again tries to write a buy order on SPOON's *keyboard.*

SPOON. Look…

This time SPOON *pushes him more forcibly but* DONNY *is stronger – he retaliates with one big aggressive shove.*

Sensing a fight, SPOON *backs away. He stands there helpless and awkward as* DONNY *write a huge buy order on his computer. Eventually* DONNY *finishes. He points to the screen to show* SPOON *what he has done and his index finger hovers over the 'Enter' button.*

DONNY. Just got to press 'Enter'. Four million.

SPOON. Donny…

DONNY. Everything you got. Stick it all on one short deal. Just say the word – I'll tap this little key for you. Gamble the whole fucking lot, Spoon. What d'ya say?

SPOON. Look…

DONNY. Haven't got the spine to do it, have you?

SPOON. No. No, I haven't. (*Pause.*) But I've got the spine to do this.

He reaches for his telephone and dials a number.

DONNY (*amused*). What? What you doing?

SPOON (*shakes his head*). I'm phoning the sixteenth. Telling them you broke your limit.

SPOON continues to dial. The phone starts to ring – he has it on speakerphone so we hear the tone.

A VOICE *answers the phone.*

VOICE. Hello?

SPOON. Compliance Director.

DONNY *slams his hand down on the receiver to silence it.*
SPOON *smiles and looks up at him.*

Now who's frightened?

Scene Nine

Restaurant.

1335hrs.

SANDY *sits alone at a restaurant table, sipping from a glass of white wine and perusing the menu.*

PJ *enters. He carries an envelope – already opened.*

He puts it on the table and SANDY *stares at it. Pause.*

SANDY. It's Barbados.

PJ. Hi.

SANDY. Shall I buy bikinis?

PJ. Sorry. Not Barbados.

SANDY. Bournemouth. Pissing Bournemouth. Oh, sod.

PJ. Not Barbados. Not Bournemouth.

SANDY. Where is it, then?

PJ. I'm happy to discuss it. But you'll need to leave a gap for me to speak.

SANDY. Paul…

He takes a large gulp from her glass.

(*Dry.*) I'll settle for a mime here, Paul. A gesture. Anything! If not Barbados, then…?

PJ. Bruges.

Pause. She stares, confused.

SANDY. We'll be going to Bruges this summer.

PJ. We can afford Bruges.

SANDY (*confused*). Bruges is more expensive than Bournemouth.

He nods.

(*Breath.*) You've got your bonus there.

He nods again.

And it's enough for us all to go to Bruges? I don't understand.

PJ (*loosens his tie*). I was first in. Some of them are still to go.

SANDY. What happened?

PJ. It's been a good year.

SANDY. Then why not Barbados?

PJ. Just listen…

SANDY. We like that hotel there – St James. And the girls – there's that nightclub on the beach…

PJ. They're underpaying me.

SANDY. What? Your bonus deal?

PJ. They're offering me less. Less than I expected.

SANDY. Why?

PJ. It's a deliberate provocation. (*Beat. Drinks.*) Shawcross is a demonic little bastard. Sits behind his desk – bald head shining in the light. I'd like to go in with a slice of bacon.

SANDY. Paul…

PJ. Great big rasher. Smack it on his head. See if it sticks.

SANDY. You're drunk already.

PJ. I am, as you say…

SANDY. Just tell me…

PJ. He underpays me – just to force me to respond. Good year – bull year – lots of money, but a meagre bonus. He wants to see which way I'm gonna jump.

Pause. She realises the weight of what he has said.

SANDY. You can't just resign. We agreed.

PJ. Yes. But what will he do then? Next year this'll be even smaller…

SANDY. But if you go now…

PJ. Exactly. I'd be starting somewhere from the bottom. Bastard's got me cornered.

Silence.

SANDY. We'll cancel our holiday.

PJ. What?

SANDY. We won't go away. Not this year. You can work the whole summer…

PJ. Sandy…

SANDY. Go in early. Start going in every day at seven o'clock. And make sure he notices…

PJ. Come on…

SANDY. We'll go out this afternoon, Paul. We'll buy you a new suit. A Paul Smith. Epsom blue.

PJ. You really think that combing my hair and buying me new underpants is going to make him reconsider, do you?

SANDY. He'll see that you're serious.

PJ. Sandy…

SANDY. Make him see. Make yourself… impossible to ignore.

PJ. 'I was thinking of edging out PJ – but now he's got a Smith suit in Epsom blue, I'm not so sure.'

SANDY. What the hell is wrong with you? Why can't you fight for what you want here? For us all. We've built a life.

PJ. We can get a cheaper kitchen.

SANDY. Paul, for Christ's sake… who do you want us to be? Me and the girls. (*Beat.*) We were going to take them away. We don't see them half the year. We planned an expensive holiday. You want them coming home this summer and finding their father camped out in front of the television?

PJ. Look…

SANDY. I don't want us to be that family. I don't want us to become… the centre of the gossip. No way. 'Poor Sandra, she's tightening her belt.' Why does it have to be our turn this year?

PJ (*holds up the letter*). Just because.

SANDY. We have dinners. You bought me sapphires. I'm not going to make do with a pair of slippers at Christmas.

PJ. What do you want me to do?

SANDY. I told you. Go back.

PJ. And accept it?

SANDY (*nods*). Next year it will be better.

   PJ *laughs*.

   What?

PJ. I'm not sure that 'next year' is an option. (*Takes a large gulp from the glass.*) I told him to shove it.

SANDY. What?

PJ. I did. There was this moment. I couldn't let it pass me by. 'Shove it up your arse.' I had to. (*Considers.*) Think I said 'arse'.

SANDY. You...

PJ. It was one of those moments in life when 'less is more', you know? I mean, I could have made a big speech. But I think that 'shove it up your arse'... it sort of encapsulated every-thing I was feeling.

SANDY. God...

PJ. I did a little mime to go with it. Nothing fancy. Just... (*He indicates his envelope-shoving mime.*) Then got up and swanned out the door.

SANDY. So that's it, then, is it? You're just doing the garden for the next forty years.

Beat.

PJ (*suddenly joyful and free, laughing*). It's the thing about marrying a trader: the shelf-life. It's something you have to bear in mind.

SANDY. Do something. Go back and apologise.

PJ. I'm hungry. Shall we order lunch? What's really cheap here?

But she is leaving.

Scene Ten

Bond floor.

1954hrs.

SPOON *sits alone at his computer. The brown envelope containing his bonus is on his lap – he reads the letter inside, not for the first time.* DONNY *comes over. He is carrying an identical envelope, already opened.* SPOON *puts his letter away.* DONNY *sits. A long game ensues.*

They look hard at each other's faces, trying to discern what might be inside the two envelopes. DONNY *tries to catch* SPOON*'s expression out of the corner of his eye…* SPOON *notices and turns away.*

Then it's SPOON*'s turn to try to catch* DONNY*'s expression. Eventually* DONNY *breaks the silence.*

DONNY. You're smiling.

SPOON. I'm not.

DONNY. I can sense it. We don't smile, Spoon. Not on bonus day. Never. (*Points.*) There's wounded here. Walking wounded. Now's not the moment for a victory parade.

SPOON. I'm *not* smiling.

DONNY. You're cheerful.

SPOON. I'm not cheerful. I'm… content.

DONNY. Well, keep it to your fucking self. Okay?

JESS *enters. She has her envelope in her hand. Silently she gathers her things.*

JESS. You boys hear about PJ?

DONNY *nods.*

Lost his temper.

DONNY. Shawcross wound him up.

JESS. Well, he fell for it. (*Beat*.) Someone's gonna have to pack his stuff up.

DONNY. This is why you're not allowed to smile.

JESS. Who's smiling?

DONNY *nods at* SPOON.

SPOON. I'm not smiling.

DONNY. He's looking content.

SPOON. ...which is a mortal sin, apparently.

DONNY. Not between the gentlemen.

JESS (*to* SPOON). Did well, did you?

DONNY. Look at his face.

JESS (*studies his face carefully and senses a smile*). Ah. You did very well.

SPOON. I did okay.

DONNY. 'Okay' doesn't grin like a tosser.

JESS. Be happy. Be happy you did well. Go out and spend your bonus. Go and buy a Lexus.

DONNY. Don't.

She stares at SPOON. *He doesn't move.*

JESS. Gonna stay, yeah? Gonna have your pissing contest? I did warn you. This is always how it starts.

DONNY (*quieter*). You want to celebrate?

JESS. Nah. I've got a date tonight.

DONNY. Anyone I know.

JESS. No. No one you know. Okay with that?

She exits. SPOON *puts on his jacket, picks up his case and exits after her. But he has left his envelope on his desk.*

DONNY notices at once but says nothing. He stares at it long and hard, not moving. Eventually he jumps to his feet and picks it up.

At that moment SPOON *comes back in to retrieve it. They look at one another in silence.* DONNY *holds it out to him.*

SPOON. Go on then, Donny.

DONNY. What?

SPOON (*amused*). 'What?' Open it. Go on.

DONNY. I didn't…

SPOON. We gonna play this game? Ever since I started making money you've been wondering. This is the first real measure. Go on.

DONNY shrugs and offers it back, trying to appear unconcerned.

DONNY. Mine is gonna be bigger.

SPOON. Mm. But by how much? That's what's killing you, isn't it?

DONNY. 'Killing' me?

SPOON. How big is the gap between us?

DONNY. Bollocks.

SPOON. How fast will it erode?

DONNY. Don't be so fucking stupid.

SPOON. Open it.

Long pause. DONNY *is just on the point of opening it. He tugs at one corner of the envelope.*

And you'll have to show me yours.

DONNY. What?

SPOON. Otherwise I'll know you think it's shit. Compared to mine.

DONNY. You arsehole…

SPOON. Not a game I can lose. If this is paltry, then so what?
That's as expected.

DONNY. You total…

SPOON. Why are you still here? Why are you still standing
here? Because you're threatened. So go on then, Donny.
Open it and look at it. Go on. Gauge the threat.

DONNY *cannot resist. They open the envelopes and gaze at
each other's bonus offer.*

Pause. We try to read their faces.

End of Act One.

ACT TWO

Scene Eleven

Trading, excerpt.

1523hrs.

DONNY, JESS *and* SPOON *are in spotlights, trading.*

JESS *is busy on the squawk.* SPOON *is tapping keys, entering the details of a trade into his computer. He eats popcorn.*

DONNY *is surly – he stares at his screen just waiting for a result. He fills a child's water pistol from a plastic bottle of water and fires it into the air.*

JESS. Jess.

VOICE 9 (*squawk, male, to* JESS). Hi. It's Rick.

JESS. Hey. What's on your mind, then, Ricky?

DONNY (*to* JESS). You. With no knickers on.

VOICE 9. Got sterling here.

JESS. Picking up my pen.

VOICE 9. One million sterling for Eurorock. Sixty-three.

JESS. I like a man who knows his own mind.

DONNY (*to* JESS). Oh, please. Spare us all.

JESS. Eurorock is spread at sixty-four.

VOICE 9. Okay. Let's park it then, shall we?

JESS. I'll call you right back, mister man. (*Hangs up and dials again.*)

DONNY. What's on his mind is a night with you in the Thistle Hotel, Docklands.

JESS. It's professional flirting.

SPOON (*hitting a key on his computer with a flourish*). We are done.

DONNY. You fuck him with your voice. You fuck him with your inflections. It's painful to listen.

JESS. Don't listen.

DONNY. He's sitting there with a teacake in his pants. I can hear the erectile tissue.

JESS. Why are you sulky?

DONNY. It's just bloody demeaning.

JESS (*to* DONNY). Says the man who spent the weekend being thrashed at golf by a client.

Irritated, DONNY *fires his water pistol at* SPOON.

SPOON (*to* DONNY). Hey!

JESS (*on the mic*). Sternly!

VOICE 10. Gonna dick up my morning, are you?

JESS. Oh, you're such a smoothie. Can we ditch the foreplay and get on?

SPOON (*to* DONNY). Nob.

He throws a handful of popcorn at DONNY.

VOICE 10. What d'you want?

JESS. Some bonds I'm thinking maybe, yeah? Eurorock. Sixty-six.

DONNY (*to* SPOON). Not getting any better with the swearing.

VOICE 10. I don't sell at sixty-six. Sorry.

DONNY. 'Go speak to your client, sternly.'

VOICE 10. Go and speak to your client, sternly.

JESS. I will.

She presses pause and wastes some time doing nothing.

SPOON (*drying his tie*). Such a prick. Got no fucking manners.

JESS. From the gutter.

DONNY (*shoots water pistol at* JESS). Hey. My family was wealthy. Big in iron and steel.

JESS. Yeah? (*On the mic.*) Sternly?

VOICE 10. Hi.

SPOON. Iron and steel?

DONNY. Yeah…

SPOON. Whatever, Donny.

JESS (*to* SPOON). His mother used to iron and his father used to steal.

DONNY (*to* JESS). You part of my act now?

JESS (*on the mic*). Can you do them at sixty-five?

VOICE 10. Er, no… Sixty-four, tops.

JESS. You ogre.

SPOON. You got it all over my tie.

DONNY. Mah.

JESS. Hey. I'm looking old before my time. I've got wrinkles 'cause of you. I'm buying shares in Olay.

SPOON. Just look.

JESS. In my book now. (*To the rest of the room, but so* VOICE 10 *can hear.*) Man drives a hard bargain…

DONNY. You crafty cow. Make him feel that he's pushing you around… (*Shouts towards* JESS*'s mic.*) Sixty-four is what you fucking wanted.

But she has hung up.

JESS. Men like to feel in charge. They like to feel like they're on top of you.

She speed-dials the squawk. It's answered quickly.

VOICE 9. Rick.

JESS. Sixty-four. Going through right now for you.

VOICE 9. Phone me when you're next up my way.

DONNY. Or down his end.

VOICE 9. Buy you lunch.

DONNY. 'And you can rummage in my pants for your bonus.'

JESS *hangs up.*

What you are is a whore.

JESS (*as if to a sulky child*). You having a bad one?

DONNY. You whore with your voice.

JESS. You having a bad day?

DONNY (*points at screen*). Fucking bonds here – Futureproof – I'm just watching them tumble.

JESS. I saw Bloomberg. Futureproof have burned.

DONNY. Yes. I'm aware.

JESS. And you went long on them! Ha! No wonder, Mr Sulky Man.

DONNY *fires the water pistol at his trading screen.*

If I'd known they were tumbling down... I could have shorted. Made a mint.

DONNY. Yeah.

JESS (*to* SPOON). Why *you* smiling?

SPOON. I did.

Silence.

DONNY. What?

SPOON. I shorted on Futureproof.

JESS. Just now?

SPOON. Yeah. Made three million six.

DONNY. You are kidding?

SPOON (*shrugs*). I got it from the internet. (*Breath. He points to his screen – an internet blog.*) Said that Futureproof was looking… wobbly. The price was gonna take a dip.

DONNY. You just made three million six?

SPOON. Bought them back when the price was down by ten.

DONNY. You made three million six?

JESS (*amused*). Oh my God, Donny. Most of that is yours.

DONNY. You made three million six on a rumour?

SPOON (*shrugs*). I read the City blogs.

JESS (*laughs*). Well, stand up. Let us applaud you.

> SPOON *obligingly stands up and bows. She applauds.*
> DONNY *bashes the desk.*

> (*To* DONNY, *appeasing him.*) You make money – someone's got to lose it.

> SPOON *sits again. Beat.* DONNY *takes his big bottle of water and empties it over* SPOON, *drenching him.*

DONNY. There. You can all applaud him now, can't you?

> DONNY *throws the water bottle across the room in a mad fury. Papers scatter.*

Scene Twelve

Bond floor.

2020hrs.

The bond floor is dark – the traders have long since gone home. A few lights twinkle in the skyscraper across the road.

DONNY *sits alone in the darkness, rifling through a pile of papers – the detritus of his day.*

JESS *enters in her coat. She carries a handbag, a briefcase and a plastic carrier bag from an off-licence.*

DONNY. Well.

JESS (*putting her stuff down*). I've never resolved the debate, you know. Handbag or briefcase. Or both.

DONNY. Sometimes it's hard to be a woman.

JESS. Go for briefcase, your make-up rattles round in it. Go for handbag and…

DONNY. …you can't fit any papers in it, no. (*Breath.*) Must be a market for briefcase-cum-handbag.

JESS. 'Swhat I'm thinking.

DONNY. Little pocket for knick-knacks. Space for your computer.

JESS. Save us girls from the appalling embarrassment of turning up to meetings with a full set of monogrammed luggage.

From her carrier she retrieves a bottle of booze and two paper cups – she starts to pour.

DONNY. Good day today?

JESS. Thank you. Yes.

DONNY. You had a good day.

JESS. And you had a rocky one.

DONNY. Beautiful euphemism. (*Breath*.) I was toast. I got toasted all over. I was wallowing in shit.

JESS. I saw Futureproof closed ten points down.

DONNY. Can you believe it? Fucking gilt-edged. Gave it to all my clients. Bloody price down by a quarter.

JESS. Rotten luck.

DONNY. Wasn't luck, it was Jesus.

JESS. Pardon?

DONNY. There was this guy busking at the station. Liverpool Street – first thing. Playing tambourine with a tape deck. Had a little sign: 'I'm busking for Jesus today. Don't give any money, just give him your immortal soul.' (*Breath*.)

JESS (*expecting the worst*). What did you do? Steal his tambourine?

DONNY. I just told him his business plan was shit.

Beat. They laugh.

Stupid cunt. 'Don't give me any money.' He could make a mint. I just thought he was ripe for a lecture.

JESS (*laughing still*). You insulted Jesus.

DONNY. I insulted his messenger. All my trading was doomed to fail. (*Beat*.) You want to celebrate? Your day.

JESS. What you thinking?

He shrugs – 'the usual'.

Ah. You don't mean 'celebrate'. You mean consolation. (*Silence. Drinks*.) You were a prick today. That stuff with Spoon.

DONNY. Couldn't stand him preening.

JESS. Couldn't stand him doing better than you. Where's it gonna end, Donny?

DONNY. Me and Spoon?

JESS. You and Spoon. You and every other prick in a chalk stripe. (*Breath*.) It's not a job – it's a fucking addiction.

DONNY. It's a race.

JESS. Damned straight.

DONNY. We're like horses.

JESS. You're like squabbling kids! You want to kick his head in after school 'cause he's better at his sums than you are. I hate watching it.

Silence. They drink.

DONNY. You been in the pub?

JESS. For a bit. Yeah.

DONNY (*smiles*). Flirting for the firm.

JESS. Don't knock it, mate. It works. (*Breath*.) It's amazing how a bloke will always get cavalier with money when presented with some girl's knockers. (*Breath. Drinks*.) Queen Elizabeth the First – she ruled a whole nation just by flirting with the boys.

DONNY. You model yourself on her, then?

JESS. I try to shake my tits in an Elizabethan way. Yes.

Her mobile buzzes. She checks her text message whilst talking.

DONNY. Why are we talking?

JESS. You just asked me…

DONNY. I mean, why are we talking? What are we doing here?

JESS. I wanted to bring you a drink.

DONNY. But you're not interested in sex, though?

JESS (*shakes her head, indicates the text*). Got to be somewhere. Sorry.

Pause. They peruse the room in silence. DONNY*'s gaze lands on* SPOON*'s chair.*

DONNY. It doesn't make you suspicious at all?

JESS. What?

DONNY. Three million six. And how long has he been here?

JESS. 'Suspicious'?

DONNY. Futureproof. Why didn't *I* see it? Why didn't *you*? Where d'you think he got his information?

JESS. Oh, I see. If he did better than you – then he must have been cheating. He looked at an internet rumour board.

DONNY. I just think…

JESS. You – you take arrogance to a whole new level. No one is allowed to be more gifted.

Beat. He leans in close.

DONNY (*a cheeky smile*). It'll be him next.

JESS. What?

DONNY. Well, you're not interested in me.

JESS. Donny…

DONNY. Has he offered to cut you in?

JESS. Christ.

DONNY. I know you.

JESS. You are something. 'Cause you can't get my knickers off…

DONNY. Is it 'cause I lost so much today?

JESS. Not even funny.

He tries to come on to her.

DONNY. One bad deal.

JESS. It's not my job to reassure you, mate.

DONNY. One bad deal – you turn me down.

JESS. This is so bloody unattractive!

DONNY. Now I'm not the biggest dick on the floor.

JESS. That's what hurts, isn't it? You think I'm some sort of scorecard.

He tries to touch her and she sidesteps him.

DONNY. He's a cheating cunt. You want a cheating cunt?

JESS. What I want is a conversation, not a 'tag' game.

DONNY. Popping round there later tonight, are you? He's the reason you're rushing off. Go on. Isn't he?

He tries to grab her phone. She pulls it away from him.

JESS. There is no one. No one preferable. I'm just not in the mood. I came to talk to you.

He stops reaching over and sits back.

DONNY. Well, thanks for your time. I'm sorry I can't offer you advancement.

JESS. I don't want to talk to you.

She heads straight for the door. He makes a lunge for her again – an ugly moment ensues. He grabs her wrist and pulls her toward him – she shoves him hard and spills drink all over him.

No. No.

And then she has gone.

Scene Thirteen

A tiny City flat.

2117hrs.

Everything is neat, precise and clinical. The owner comes here to sleep and occasionally to eat – nothing more.

SPOON *is in his shirtsleeves – just in from work. He holds his dinner on a tray: a microwave meal and a can of Coke.*

JESS *has come to visit him. She stands in her coat, carrying her briefcase.*

SPOON. Having dinner.

  He gestures her into the room.

JESS. This is where you live?

SPOON. You like?

JESS (*softly, smiles*). It's… Well. Kind of compact. One room.

SPOON. Two. Toilet in there. (*Shrugs.*) Five minutes from the DLR. It's not all that expensive.

JESS. Well, good. Since you can't actually lie down in here.

  He laughs a little.

SPOON. You want something?

JESS. Like?

SPOON. A drink?

JESS. Why don't we find a pub? Oxygen might run out – with two of us in here.

SPOON. Are you okay?

JESS. What d'you mean?

SPOON. Look like you've had 'a day'.

JESS. Oh, you know. Lose a million. Make a million.

SPOON. Yeah.

He sits with her.

JESS. I'd have thought you were a 'rolling plains' type. Stables and a paddock down in Sussex. Isn't this a bit... urban?

SPOON (*shrugs*). Eat and sleep here. You figure, 'What's the point?' If I'm gonna put the hours in... just need a mattress.

Beat.

JESS. You don't entertain in here?

SPOON. You're it. You're the first. Who would come?

JESS (*looks around her*). Seven dwarves, possibly. (*Breath.*) You had a good day.

SPOON (*holding up his food*). Tesco Finest.

JESS. What?

SPOON. Tesco Finest. This is me splashing out. Celebrating.

Beat. She puts her bags down.

JESS. I saw Donny.

SPOON (*laughs*). He was reeling, I bet.

JESS. He's feeling sore. (*Gentle smile.*) Just warning you.

SPOON (*half-laugh*). You think he's gonna get me at playtime?

JESS. I'm saying I was with him just now. He's in an... ugly mood.

SPOON (*dry*). Well, Jeez. That's hard to imagine.

JESS. Can't stay at the top of your game. Someone better always comes along. (*Half-breath.*) And after today...

SPOON (*laughs with derision*). Of course. He thinks I'm the usurper...

JESS. Got your text. (*Breath.*) Why did you need to see me, Ollie?

Beat. He reaches into his jacket pocket and produces an envelope. She opens it. There is a printed card inside.

SPOON. I got this. Internal mail.

JESS (*reads it and smiles*). 'Girton Manor.'

SPOON. What is it?

JESS. It's an invitation.

SPOON. Yeah. Sure…

JESS. It's a weekend in the country. A conference. They put us into little teams – brainstorm company strategy.

SPOON. Ah.

JESS. Last year they made guacamole. One of you holds the avocado and the other the spoon. (*Unconvinced.*) Helps create a corporate identity.

SPOON. It's not… sinister in any way?

JESS. Sorry?

SPOON. Asking me to go.

JESS. It's a jolly. Get everyone to 'bond'. Of course, the only real bonding that goes on all weekend is everyone's lips bonding with Sir David's arsehole. Why on earth would you think it was sinister?

SPOON. I'm leaving.

Silence.

JESS. You're leaving the bank?

SPOON. I've got an offer. Yes.

JESS. To leave?

SPOON. Did you see Bloomberg? You saw the news today. Shads.

JESS. Expanding.

SPOON. Dutch bank.

JESS. Yes. I know who they are.

SPOON. They're creating… well, a new department.

JESS. They approached you?

SPOON. My father… (*Silence.*) I thought maybe – this weekend away – I thought maybe that they knew. That this was some kind of sweetener.

She shakes her head.

'Cause if they knew about it…

JESS. I understand. Yeah.

SPOON. I'd get fired. Before I could resign. Lose everything I've got. Lose all my stock – my pension. Lose my clients – obviously I want to take them with me. Picking up and going to another bank – it's not all that easy. You have to be… discreet.

JESS. It's 'cause of Donny.

SPOON. What?

JESS. I understand. He's been a prick.

SPOON. No. No.

JESS. I understand.

SPOON. Do you really think that I'm skulking away?

He produces a letter from his pocket. He puts it in front of her: a job offer.

One million guaranteed bonus. And a title. 'Desk Head.'

JESS (*reading*). This is a promotion, then. Bravo.

She hands the paper back to him.

You really texted me… you dragged me across town tonight just to have someone to tell?

SPOON. I dragged you across town tonight so I could talk about careers, Jess. They want to build a whole new team.

Silence. She looks at him.

JESS (*half-laugh*). You're offering me a job?

SPOON. Are you interested?

JESS. At Shads?

SPOON. One million guaranteed basic – for the first two years.

JESS. Look…

SPOON. I need you to come with me.

JESS. You *need* me?

SPOON. They want us *all*. The trading team. Ten guys. Telecoms and media.

Silence.

JESS. I don't understand…

SPOON. Yeah, you do. I am appointed as the new Head of Department. Provided… I can bring along with me every single one of my colleagues. From the team at McSorley's.

Silence.

JESS. You need me to persuade the guys?

SPOON. They don't know me. They don't trust me.

JESS. No.

SPOON. Not as much as you.

JESS. Uh-huh. So you need me. You need me to recruit for you. To do all the dirty stuff.

SPOON (*suddenly less affable*). I need you to make a decision.

Beat.

JESS. I don't… Look, Ollie…

SPOON. One million sterling. Over the first two years. That enough to get you on board?

JESS. You're not just asking me to leave – you're asking me to strip the place bare.

SPOON. One million. That's huge. (*Steps in closer.*) Seven resignations. Get me seven resignations. We all go. As a team.

JESS. Eight.

SPOON. Not Donny. I'll take all the others. But not him.

Beat.

JESS. If he found out...

SPOON. There's risk in everything that matters.

Silence. She is deciding.

And then she takes off her coat. She is staying to talk more.

Scene Fourteen

Suburban garden.

1410hrs.

DONNY *has come to visit* PJ*'s home. He sits in the garden with a mug of tea. His BlackBerry is lying on the table in front of him.*

DONNY *looks tired and dishevelled.* SANDY *enters with a plate of biscuits.*

DONNY. Saw the sign.

SANDY. Yes.

DONNY. The house is up for sale.

SANDY. We're going to Hove. Well... we plan to.

DONNY. What's in Hove?

SANDY. Well, we are. (*Beat.*) He wants to buy a boat. They have a marina.

DONNY. What's he going to do with a boat?

SANDY. I can't honestly imagine.

Beat. She sits. He takes a biscuit.

DONNY. Hove is nice.

SANDY. You've been?

DONNY. I went for a stag do.

SANDY. Ah. So you can vouch for the beer.

DONNY. And the strippers. Yes, I can.

He smiles. She doesn't.

SANDY. Paul has his eye on an oast house. Apparently Sussex is full of them.

DONNY. An 'oast house'?

SANDY. You know. Can't imagine how you hang up wallpaper. And hoovering must be a nightmare. All the walls – curved.

DONNY. Sounds nice. Little oast house.

SANDY. I don't really want… our lounge suite fits perfectly here.

Silence.

You're one of the oldest.

DONNY. I don't understand.

SANDY. You've been at McSorley's a while.

DONNY. Ten years.

SANDY. Donald. Yes?

DONNY. Donny.

SANDY. He says these names. Said.

DONNY. We really don't know each other.

SANDY. You worked together.

DONNY. Same room. Not 'together', though.

SANDY. No. (*Beat.*) I know there's always younger people. Come on to the floor. Cut into the bonus pool.

DONNY. I'm not the reason you're moving to Hove.

SANDY. No?

DONNY. I haven't taken your mortgage payment.

SANDY. Not personally. (*Breath.*) I understand. But it's hard not to look at you and think…

DONNY. …about them divvying up the money.

SANDY. Paul didn't get as much as he hoped. Means someone else got more. Small wonder you don't get close.

Beat.

DONNY (*remembering*). You used to work in the City.

SANDY (*nods*). Client services. Four years.

DONNY. You know what it's like?

SANDY. Yes.

DONNY (*half-laugh*). Sorry. Hard to picture you.

SANDY. I once took some clients out to a strip club; the girls stood in showers and soaped themselves.

DONNY *laughs*.

The clients all fired at their tits with water pistols. Got an image now?

DONNY. Gosh.

SANDY. Can't say I enjoyed my whole time. But a woman has to play a part.

DONNY. I suppose.

SANDY. No 'suppose' about it. 'Risk' is what little boys do.

PJ enters. He wears a casual shirt, a sweater and cords. He looks relaxed and healthy.

PJ. Estate agent.

SANDY. What did he say?

PJ (*shakes his head*). It's way too expensive. Not in our price range.

SANDY (*nods toward* DONNY – *'not in front of the servants'*). Paul. (*To* DONNY.) Would you excuse me, Donald? I'm clearing out the larder. Found sardines from 1990.

She smiles and exits.

DONNY. She's pissed off.

PJ. Had her heart set on a kitchen. Already chosen the cabinets.

DONNY. But you're okay?

PJ. Girls at uni. Pension. Stock options. We're not going to starve. Sardines keep for years, you know.

DONNY. I know they do.

Beat.

PJ. Just 'cause an eighteenth-century oast house is out of our range, I don't think we qualify as paupers.

Beat.

DONNY. She thinks that I'm the one. The reason you got pushed down the bottom of the food chain.

PJ. She's an expensive wife. Anything less than seven bedrooms is… penury. Had to swagger to win her in the first place. Splashed out on sapphires. Weekends at hotels. The trouble with pretending to be flash – she soon gets used to the life. And then you're stuck. (*He stares at* DONNY.) You look thinner.

Beat. DONNY *shrugs.*

How much d'you lose?

DONNY (*shrugs*). Nah. One bad trade.

PJ. And then what? (*Breath. No answer.*) Risk limit got slashed?

DONNY *nods*.

How much was it?

DONNY. I'm nine million down.

PJ. Shit.

DONNY. Long and wrong on Futureproof – I don't need to tell you, do I? (*Breath.*) Spoon was lucky. He shorted it.

PJ. Woah. He's got talent, then?

DONNY. Maybe he has.

PJ. I know that look, Donny. Nine million down is no time to get competitive, matey. It's a time to be cautious – to pause. You're gonna risk your job, chasing the top spot.

DONNY. Well, thanks, Yoda. I'm glad you've had the ears taken care of. (*Pause. Drinks.*)

PJ. Remember Alf?

DONNY. Aggressive little fucker.

PJ. Even he. Thirty-two. Chucked out on his ear.

DONNY. Uh-huh.

PJ. Remember how we beat our breasts for him? How's he gonna cope?

DONNY. I don't think I went quite that far.

PJ. The guy got out when he was thirty-two. Had years ahead of him. Don't you think he was the lucky one?

DONNY. PJ...

PJ. What's the alternative? At the chalk face 'til you're fifty then retire and find the kids have disowned you.

DONNY*'s BlackBerry starts to buzz.*

When did you last see your kid? When did you last take your
boy to… Windsor Castle?

DONNY. I took him into work last year. Sat him on my lap and
let him make a thousand pounds. (*Takes his BlackBerry.*) Do
you mind?

He checks the message. PJ *is frowning.*

(*To* PJ.) What?

PJ. I was giving you advice there.

DONNY. I'm listening.

PJ. I had more to say.

DONNY. Really? Spiffing.

PJ. You want to put that away?

DONNY *reaches into his bag and pulls out his laptop – he is
going to make a trade.*

DONNY. Have you got wireless?

PJ (*gestures to the computer*). Turn that thing off.

DONNY. No.

PJ. Turn it off.

DONNY. Fuck off.

PJ. Don't talk that way to me. I'm trying to help here.

PJ *steals his laptop from under his nose and shuts it.*
DONNY *tries, unsuccessfully, to grab it.*

Let's have a proper conversation.

DONNY. My concern for you has totally buggered off now.

PJ. Just you and me.

DONNY. And if I do will you give me that thing back?

PJ *nods.*

(*Sighs.*) You're costing me thousands. You arsehole.

PJ. You used to take the piss. All of you. I know you did. 'PJ rattling on about nothing.' But you needed me – you didn't know it at the time. I humanised you. (*Breath.*) Two minutes, Donny. Now, please.

DONNY *stops trying to grab the computer and leans back in his chair, ready to converse.*

Engage me in conversation.

DONNY. What do you want to talk about?

Beat.

PJ. What you did on your holidays.

DONNY. I didn't go on holiday.

PJ. No. Of course. I went to Dorset last week. Been there?

DONNY. I may have. (*Breath.*)

PJ. Corfe Castle. Beautiful tearooms.

DONNY. Right, well, I'll be sure and pay a visit. Schedule some time.

He tries to reach for the laptop. PJ *whisks it away again.*

PJ. Global warming. Is it a myth?

DONNY. What?

PJ. What's your take?

DONNY. This is insane. What's this got to do with anything?

PJ. What's your position on global warming?

DONNY. I could be making money now.

PJ. This is important. (*Breath.*)

DONNY. Someone's employing you, aren't they? One of my competitors is employing you to distract me.

PJ. China is industrialising. Is this a threat to our planet?

PJ *leaves a long silence for* DONNY *to respond.*

DONNY *has nothing to say.*

No? Okay then. (*Breath.*) Tony Hancock. Is he funny?

DONNY. Why you asking me?

PJ. You know who Hancock is?

DONNY. I think so.

PJ. Is he funny?

DONNY. I s'pose.

PJ. Why?

Silence. DONNY *is looking bemused.*

You're like one of those laboratory rats. You'd die in the wild if you were set free.

DONNY. I'm dying right now.

PJ. When you see your kid – what do you two talk about? I bet I can guess.

Scene Fifteen

Trading, excerpt.

1125hrs.

The trading floor is up and running: SPOON, DONNY *and* JESS *in spotlights.*

DONNY *speaks in a loud whisper – anxious that his current deal does not get too much publicity.*

DONNY. Teleset.

SPOON. You got a price?

JESS. Arigato.

VOICE 11 (*to* DONNY). Do you wanna bail?

DONNY. I'm selling on.

VOICE 12 (*to* SPOON). At oh-point-five.

DONNY. All over the net.

SPOON. Be like Wall's.

VOICE 12. Wall's?

SPOON. Diversify.

DONNY. The rumours say we hit.

SPOON. Make money winter and summer. Ice creams and sausages.

JESS *presses her squawk again.*

JESS. I've got BT at one-oh-nine and holding here.

VOICE 11. Okay, let's shift it.

VOICE 12. Three-quarters.

VOICE 13 (*to* JESS). Yep. Let's lift it.

JESS. Yours at two-point-one.

JESS *and* SPOON *start writing orders on their computers.*
DONNY *kisses the screen.*

DONNY. Yes. Yes. I am so fucking fucking back.

SPOON (*to* JESS, *referring to* DONNY). What's up with...?

JESS (*to* SPOON). He's stopped eating moody beans for breakfast.

DONNY. Woah! Yeah!

DONNY *jumps to his feet and dances in front of* SPOON.

A little rumour... A gorgeous little internet rumour.

JESS. You got something sweet?

DONNY. Teleset. Launching a new bond.

JESS. Uh-huh. And that's why you're shagging your screen, is it?

DONNY. If they're launching a new bond the old ones will die.

SPOON. You're going short?

DONNY. Eight million!

JESS. Donny!

SPOON. Eight? In one deal!?

DONNY. You got to play to win.

JESS. You stuck eight million quid on one short? (*Answers her squawk*.) Call you back.

SPOON. You're fucking nuts.

DONNY. I am the King of You.

SPOON (*face falling*). Uh-huh? And that's the point, I guess.

JESS. I thought they slashed your limit. What you doing?

SPOON *starts to surf the internet – looking for the bulletin*.

DONNY. Oh, what are you? My mother now?

JESS*'s squawk is ringing again. She answers it.*

JESS. Call you back. (*To* DONNY.) You sure about it?

DONNY. Got it from a rumour board. (*To* SPOON.) Yes – I read them too! They launch a new bond – their old ones will dip.

JESS. Yes, but… Eight million you don't own.

DONNY. I'll buy them all back by teatime! Every shag in here is going to be clamouring.

JESS. You're trying to get back on top in one short deal?

DONNY. A new bond! The old ones will dive down. You watch me whip his Spoony bum right now!

SPOON (*reading the screen*). Except it isn't a new bond.

Silence.

JESS. What?

SPOON. Look at the internet. Teleset press launch. It isn't a new bond.

JESS. What?

SPOON. It's a new microchip that they're launching. (*He laughs hard.*) All the old bonds will soar, you fucking imbecile.

DONNY. Shitting fuck.

SPOON. You've got to buy eight million for your client. By five o'clock.

JESS (*reading her screen*). No.

SPOON (*with delight*). It's such a thin line, Donny – between being early on a deal, and being wrong.

DONNY (*hammering the keys of his keyboard*). Fuck. Fuck!

SPOON. Where the hell are you gonna start? Buying back eight million that you've already sold?

JESS (*to* SPOON). Christ! Don't keep on.

DONNY *pushes* SPOON *to one side so he can read his screen.*

DONNY. Fuck.

SPOON. I can always help you out if you want.

DONNY. What?

SPOON. Help you out – just if you're stuck.

JESS (*reading her screen*). Look. The price is soaring, Donny.

DONNY (*to* SPOON). You got Teleset you can sell me? How
    much?

SPOON (*sneers*). No, I haven't. But I'm happy to lend you a
    tenner. Just for cabs.

    *DONNY looks ready to punch him. JESS stands between
    them.*

    *Silence. They stare. The squawk boxes are ringing all around
    them.*

Scene Sixteen

Bond floor.

0712hrs.

*SPOON arrives for work. He commences his regular routine of
removing his coat and booting up his computer. His trading
screen appears. He checks his e-mails, rummages in his pocket
for change and exits.*

*On the way out of the door he notices DONNY's jacket slung
over a chair.*

*DONNY enters in his shirtsleeves. He carries an empty card-
board box. Silently he starts to clear his belongings into his desk.*

*He hears a footfall. SPOON enters with a Styrofoam cup of
coffee and a bar of chocolate. He stops for a moment and looks
at DONNY, then sits at his computer and begins work. He
dunks the chocolate in his coffee and eats it.*

SPOON. So. Clearing out our desk today, then?

DONNY. Always been sharp, Spoon, haven't you? Yes. Pas-
    tures new. Shawcross isn't a total ogre, but he can't overlook
    my losses. Not any more.

SPOON. He fired you.

DONNY. Why aren't you smiling? He was succinct. 'Fuck off to another firm.' (*Beat*.) Five words. Got to admire his economy. (*Breath*.) Could have said it quicker, I suppose. Could have said it in two.

He recommences packing his stuff. SPOON *watches*.

You want to crow – this is your moment.

SPOON. Can I have your mouse mat? If you don't need it.

DONNY. There you go.

SPOON (*rummages for change*). Oh, and if you're going past the vendor…

DONNY. Sure. What d'you want? A Twix?

SPOON. If you're not too busy. Or a Yorkie.

He holds out the change – a malevolent smile.

DONNY *stares back*.

DONNY. Can I ask you one thing? Before I go. (*Breath*.)

SPOON (*impatient*). Well?

DONNY. That deal you made. Futureproof…

SPOON. Really burned you, didn't it, Donny?

DONNY *perches on the desk very close to him*.

DONNY. First big deal. Three million six. Why did you choose it?

SPOON (*turns away; dismissive*). I got it from a rumour board.

DONNY. Right. (*Breath*.) Kind of risky.

SPOON. Well…

DONNY. Three million six – all on a rumour.

SPOON. Well. Maybe.

DONNY. Anyone could have posted it. You must have done some… analysis.

SPOON. Oh, sure.

DONNY. So… what made you buy it?

SPOON. The price was about to fall. Obviously.

Beat.

DONNY (*leans in, speaking softly*). I know the price was about to fall. That's how you earned your money. But how did you know?

SPOON. I made a profit!

DONNY. That's not what I'm asking.

SPOON. Look. Their earnings are bad.

DONNY. What are their earnings?

SPOON. They're bad.

DONNY. And? What are they? (*Breath.*) If you're gonna go short on something you have to be rock solid that it's gonna go under. What made you sell Futureproof, Spoon?

SPOON. Donny…

DONNY. Little angels swooped down from heaven and whispered?

Silence.

SPOON. I already said. Their earnings are bad.

DONNY. So. What are their earnings?

SPOON. Some journalist was saying in the press.

DONNY. Who? (*Breath.*)

SPOON. I don't know his name.

DONNY. Well, what article?

SPOON. I took a quick peep at their profile.

DONNY. And? What did it say?

Silence.

SPOON. That their earnings are bad.

Silence.

DONNY. Do you play golf?

SPOON. Look, I've got somewhere that I need to be.

DONNY. Do you? Do you like to play?

SPOON *shakes his head.*

No. I knew that. I knew you didn't like to play. Golf – right –
is a self-regulating game. You cheat at golf and no one will
play with you. The same with us – a man who cheats at golf
cheats the market.

SPOON. I got lucky.

He tries to stand up and walk away. DONNY *pushes him
down again quite forcibly.*

DONNY. Don't start with me, you little stoat.

SPOON. What?

DONNY. We can do this really quickly. We can do it right now.
(*Looks at his watch.*) Quarter past seven exactly. Pretty soon
the room is gonna fill up with people. You want to spin this
out 'til then, do you? We're going to have this conversation.
I want to know everything.

SPOON. Look, Donny…

DONNY. Three million six? Some numpty puts it on his blog
and you think, 'Ooh, this'll do.'

SPOON. It was instinct.

DONNY. Oh, was it? Fucking instinct.

SPOON. You… people get a feel for things.

DONNY. People do. But not you.

SPOON. Donny…

DONNY. Look at those creases in your trousers. You spend hours pressing those with a steam iron. That's precision, that is.

SPOON (*anxious that they will be heard*). Can we…?

DONNY. You're not a guy who runs on instinct. You're a guy who has his laundry routine meticulously planned. You're cautious – you're a cautious little cunt. Christ – you keep a fucking stack of paper napkins in that drawer! So. Don't sit there talking crap about 'instinct'. Tell me now. Or you can wait until the audience arrives.

A very long pause.

DONNY *checks his watch.*

Seven sixteen.

Another long pause. He looks again.

Seventeen.

SPOON. My flatmate…

DONNY. What?

SPOON. Not here. I live alone. I meant Hong Kong – when I was training.

DONNY. He's back in London.

SPOON. Working at a newspaper.

DONNY. You send him stuff.

SPOON. I sent him… I told him…

DONNY. *You* started the rumour. (*Silence.*) Pick off some weakling company; kill it with gossip and ride the wave on the way down…

SPOON. Donny…

DONNY. What'd you do?

SPOON. He's got... he's got contacts.

DONNY. He can pick up the phone to a dozen banks and spread the word. (*Breath.*) Go on. You want to tell me, don't you? How clever you've been. There was no poxy rumour board.

SPOON. I sold the bonds. I shorted. I sold them first.

DONNY. And...

SPOON. He got on the phone – told everyone to sell.

DONNY. The price plummeted. And you bought them back.

SPOON. Yes.

DONNY. Three million six. I've got to admire your restraint, you know. Three million six. 'Sa good number. If it had been more than that someone might have been on to you. (*Beat.*) Tsk. Tsk. And you a student at Jesus. And a rowing blue.

SPOON. How did you know?

DONNY. I didn't know.

SPOON *stares at him – angry and bewildered.*

I just thought if you'd been a bit clever then you'd want to tell someone. You'd want to just... savour it.

SPOON. Look, Donny...

DONNY (*gets very close now; threatening*). Desperate to race me, weren't you? Desperate to nose ahead.

SPOON. You kind of threw down the gauntlet! You had me holding some polish and a duster within three fucking minutes of being in the room. Of course I was gonna take a chance! Of course I was gonna try anything. You were goading me! You can't start coming on like Jesus because I fucking scammed you. You're the one who started it, you goblin.

DONNY *punches* SPOON *hard in the face.*

A fight erupts. SPOON *retaliates and punches* DONNY, *but his punch is ineffectual. They grapple like little children, their rivalry finally erupting into violence. Papers fly.* DONNY *eventually throws* SPOON *to the floor and kicks him viciously.*

Silence. They stand there, panting.

SPOON *gets up and clutches a handkerchief to his bleeding nose.*

We can't keep this under wraps, I suppose?

DONNY *grabs the end of* SPOON's *tie and pulls his face very close.*

DONNY (*aggressive whisper*). I'd love to take out a full-page ad in the *FT*. 'Trash and Cash.' Would make such a great parting shot.

SPOON *is confused. He tries to read* DONNY's *expression.*

SPOON. You're not going to shop me?

DONNY. It's not burgeoning friendship that's stopping me.

SPOON. Donny…

DONNY. I'd love to phone up your old man and tell him all about you – no talent. Just a posh prick in a tie. You'd be out on your arse, on the pavement. You'd never get a City job again.

SPOON (*reads* DONNY's *face*). But… you're not going to.

DONNY. Imagine that.

Angrily, DONNY *picks up his box and heads for the door.*

Scene Seventeen

Bond floor.

0745hrs.

JESS *arrives and sits down at her desk to write a short letter. In silence she reads it back and then seals it in an envelope.*

SPOON *arrives next. He has cleaned up his face and dusted down his clothes. He is trying hard not to look as though he has been in a brutal fight this morning. They speak in an urgent whisper.*

SPOON. You've got them? Seven.

JESS. Got them.

SPOON. Seven resignations?

JESS. Got them.

She reaches into her briefcase and produces a pile of seven envelopes.

Eight. Put mine in there too.

SPOON. Eight.

JESS. Nine with your one.

SPOON. Yes. Nine.

JESS. You got yours, have you?

SPOON (*taps his jacket pocket*). Got mine here.

JESS. And when we meeting?

SPOON. Eight o'clock. On the sixteenth floor. Breakfast with Sir Dave.

He reaches out his hand for the envelopes. She pauses and will not offer them.

Shall I have those?

JESS. What happened with Donny?

SPOON. What?

JESS. This morning. What happened with Donny?

SPOON. Have you seen him?

JESS. No. What happened? (*Breath*.)

SPOON. He was fired.

JESS. You had a row. You were seen. Now everyone's gossiping about it.

SPOON. Yes. He hit me. He was fired. (*Beat*.) Shall I take those?

JESS. He just hit you?

SPOON. Look, we need to go…

JESS. You're sounding kind of casual about it, Ollie. Like you expected it.

SPOON. He was angry. He'd been fired. I made a comment.

JESS. What d'you say?

SPOON. I called him a 'goblin'.

JESS. And he hit you?

SPOON. He was angry. Shall I take them?

Pause. She doesn't move.

Shall I take those?

JESS. Do you mind if I hang on to them?

SPOON. Why?

JESS. Well – I just want to.

SPOON. We're resigning. We're supposed to be resigning.

JESS. I can hold them. When we go into the meeting.

SPOON. You don't want me to hold them? The resignation letters.

JESS. No. I don't.

Silence. He looks at her expression.

SPOON. Is there suddenly an issue of trust?

JESS. Well, actually…

SPOON. There is? There's a trust problem?

JESS. I like the way you say it. 'An issue of trust.' 'A trust problem.' 'The trust-factor's missing.'

SPOON. You're saying you don't trust me.

JESS. Fucking bull's-eye.

SPOON. Jess…

JESS. What happened with Donny? (*Breath.*)

SPOON. He got fired. He was twenty million down.

JESS. I meant what happened between you two.

Beat.

SPOON. He doesn't like me.

JESS. No. He calls you a 'cunt'.

SPOON. Yes.

JESS. A 'cheating cunt'. But this time he hit you. Why did he do that?

Beat.

SPOON. I'm not.

JESS. What?

SPOON. I'm not a cheat.

JESS. He got the 'cunt' part right?

SPOON. If he thought I'd done something illegal he'd tell the whole world. (*He immediately regrets this choice of word.*)

JESS. 'Illegal'?

SPOON. I just…

JESS. What a word to use.

SPOON (*looks at his watch*). We really have to go. One million guaranteed.

JESS. Great. It's going to be Disneyland.

He reaches over to take the letters. She won't let go of them.

Both of their hands rest on the stack of resignation envelopes.

I just want you to convince me first that my new boss isn't just a guy whose reputation's built on lies.

Beat. Finally he pulls the envelopes away from her.

SPOON. I'm a golfer.

JESS. What?

SPOON. A man can't get a partner if he cheats.

JESS. You're a golfer?

SPOON. Yes.

JESS. Oh fine, then. You've certainly convinced me.

SPOON. How do I know that I can trust *you*?

JESS. What?

SPOON. Convince me I can trust *you*.

JESS. I just put my career in your hands there.

SPOON. You could have phoned Sir David already. Told him my plans.

JESS (*playing along*). Yes.

SPOON. This envelope here could be empty. Comes a point when you have to trust someone.

JESS. And since you're a golfer, well…

SPOON. Shall we go up? We are expected.

She smiles and steps a little closer. We are certain she is about to agree. And then…

JESS. Tell me what the fight was about. If you want me to come – you have to tell me. I insist on knowing.

SPOON. Jess…

JESS. I've heard Donny whining on for weeks now – telling me exactly what you are. And I thought it was… hubris. I thought he was just feeling bruised. Then I come in and hear about this morning.

SPOON. Jess…

JESS. Got to ask yourself why. Got to ask yourself what would make Donny throw a punch in your direction.

SPOON. He was mad.

JESS. Because you called him a 'goblin'.

Beat. He has no answer for her.

I realised the truth about you, Ollie, before I even wrote that letter of resignation – before I sealed the envelope this morning. I knew Donny was right. Something happened between you. And now I've got to decide if I should let you govern my career.

SPOON (*indicates letter*). It's already decided.

JESS is inscrutable. Silence.

Something about her silence makes SPOON nervous.

He looks at her resignation letter and suddenly tears it open.

Inside is a blank piece of paper. He turns it over in his hands and his face falls. Silence again.

In a panic he starts to open the other seven letters. He opens every single one. Every one contains a blank piece of paper. He drops them to the floor.

SPOON. I can't go. Not without the team. I told the bank…

JESS. You can't stay here.

SPOON. Why? (*Breath. She smiles.*) You told him. Shawcross knows.

JESS (*nods*). Uh-huh. (*Breath.*) I told him. He's going to fire you right now.

SPOON. Before I can resign. That means…

JESS. You probably won't get breakfast. Still, there's a van on the corner that does breakfast baps. Two pounds. Sausage, egg and bacon. You should be able to afford that, still.

SPOON (*lost for words*). I…

JESS. He's agreed to up my salary. For… loyalty, I think was his reason.

Scene Eighteen

Fast-food restaurant.

1935hrs.

SEAN *eats his burger and fries.* DONNY *sits opposite and watches him.*

SEAN. I told him about what you do. (*Another mouthful.*) I said about trading.

DONNY. Who's Joshy?

SEAN. My new best friend. (*Beat.*) He's come from another school. His dad does computers. And his mum does science in a hospital.

DONNY (*uncomfortable*). And you told him about what I do.

SEAN. I told him you make eight million quid a day.

DONNY. Well.

An embarrassed pause. SEAN *eats.*

SEAN. His dad doesn't make as much as that.

DONNY. No.

SEAN. You make most. Of all the dads.

DONNY. What else shall we talk about…? (*Beat.*) Sorry about last week. (*Breath.*) Chained to the desk. You know.

SEAN. 'Time-short, cash-rich.'

DONNY. Yeah.

SEAN (*reciting without feeling*). 'Can buy a Van Gogh, but what's the point if you never even get a chance to look at it?'

Pause. DONNY *stares at him.*

DONNY. Something that Mum says?

SEAN *nods.*

Okay. Right. Fine. She's not bitter, then. (*Beat.*) Thing is, I've got some free time. I mean, we can spend some time. I don't have to work. (*Breath.*)

SEAN. What's happened?

DONNY. Nothing. Well… something. Call it a holiday. I thought we could visit a castle.

SEAN *shrugs at the suggestion – unimpressed.*

You don't like castles.

SEAN. Did you like castles?

DONNY. I never really went to one. I thought we could find one.

SEAN *isn't listening.*

How are things at school? How's Dylan?

SEAN. I don't sit with him any more.

DONNY. Really?

SEAN. You told me. That I shouldn't. So I don't.

DONNY. Well. Sort of.

SEAN. I sit with Joshy. His dad does computers.

DONNY. You said.

Another awkward pause. DONNY *wants to say something, but then chooses not to.*

You want some more nuggets? Let me get you some nuggets.

SEAN. I've got money here.

DONNY. I can buy you nuggets.

SEAN. I've got money here.

DONNY. No, Sean. You don't have to pay for your own dinner.

SEAN digs out a small pocket-money purse. It is bulging.

Woah.

SEAN. I opened a shop. In my bedroom.

DONNY. What d'you sell?

SEAN. My drawings and stuff. I sell them to Nan.

DONNY. She actually offers you money?

SEAN. I lay 'em out on my duvet with a price tag.

DONNY. Ah.

SEAN. Pictures of me and Nan. She thinks they're cute. She gets out her purse.

DONNY (*commending him*). Know your market.

Beat. SEAN *is grinning.*

What?

SEAN. Sometimes I bring other people's pictures home from school. Nan doesn't know. She still pays for them.

DONNY. Right. (*Breath.*) All this because of what I said?

SEAN. I'm making loads.

DONNY. Oh, goody. By fleecing your nan.

SEAN *takes out his money and starts to count it, gleefully.*

(*Mutters.*) 'Scumbag.' You know that word? 'Scumbag'?

SEAN. What?

DONNY. I thought it was just one of those made-up words. (*Almost to himself.*) Turns out it's a real concept. 'Scumbag.' Wanna know how I know it's real?

SEAN. Sorry?

DONNY *reaches over and touches his son's hands to stop him counting.*

DONNY. Let's talk about something else. Let's talk about castles.

SEAN. What?

DONNY. I want to have a conversation.

Fade.

The End.

A Nick Hern Book

Roaring Trade first published in Great Britain as a paperback original in 2009 by Nick Hern Books Limited, 14 Larden Road, London W3 7ST, in association with Soho Theatre, London

Roaring Trade copyright © 2009 Steve Thompson

Steve Thompson has asserted his right to be identified as the author of this work

Cover photograph: Hugo Glendinning
Cover design: Ned Hoste, 2H

Typeset by Nick Hern Books, London
Printed and bound in Great Britain by CPI Antony Rowe, Chippenham, Wiltshire

A CIP catalogue record for this book is available from the British Library

ISBN   978 1 84842 040 3

FSC
Mixed Sources
Product group from well-managed
forests and other controlled sources
Cert no. SGS-COC 2953
www.fsc.org
© 1996 Forest Stewardship Council